RUSSIA'S CHECHEN WARS 1994-2000

Lessons from Urban Combat

Olga Oliker

Prepared for the United States Army

Approved for public release; distribution unlimited

Arroyo Center
RAND

The research described in this report was sponsored by the United States Army under Contract DASW01-96-C-0004.

Library of Congress Cataloging-in-Publication Data

Oliker, Olga.
  Russia's Chechen wars 1994–2000 : lessons from urban combat / Olga Oliker.
    p. cm.
  "MR-1289."
  Includes bibliographical references.
  ISBN 0-8330-2998-3
    1. Chechnëï (Russia)—History—Civil War, 1994– 2. Urban warfare—Russia
  (Federation)—Chechnëï.

  DK511.C37 O44 2001
  947.086—dc21

                                                                    2001041627

Cover photo credit: "Grozny, Ville Rayee de la Carte," French photographer Eric Bouvet. Courtesy AFP PHOTO. Reprinted by permission.

RAND is a nonprofit institution that helps improve policy and decisionmaking through research and analysis. RAND® is a registered trademark. RAND's publications do not necessarily reflect the opinions or policies of its research sponsors.

Published 2001 by RAND
1700 Main Street, P.O. Box 2138, Santa Monica, CA 90407-2138
1200 South Hayes Street, Arlington, VA 22202-5050
201 North Craig Street, Suite 102, Pittsburgh, PA 15213-1516
RAND URL: http://www.rand.org/
To order RAND documents or to obtain additional information,
contact Distribution Services: Telephone: (310) 451-7002;
Fax: (310) 451-6915; Internet: order@rand.org

PREFACE

This report provides an analysis of Russian combat in Chechnya beginning with the first modern Chechen war of 1994–1996 and comparing and contrasting it with the ongoing conflict that began in 1999. While the focus is on combat in urban areas, more general aspects of the Chechnya wars are also discussed. The research reported here was initiated with the goal of better understanding what Russia's urban experience in Chechnya indicates both about Russian capabilities and operations specifically and about urban warfare generally, with lessons to be drawn for other states, including, of course, the United States.

This effort was undertaken as a component of a project on military operations on urbanized terrain. The project was co-sponsored by the Office of the Deputy Assistant Secretary of the Army for Research and Technology and the Office of the Deputy Chief of Staff for Intelligence, U.S. Army. The project was conducted jointly in the Force Development and Technology Program and the Strategy, Doctrine, and Resources Program of RAND Arroyo Center, a federally funded research and development center sponsored by the United States Army. It should be of interest to policymakers and analysts concerned with the operational aspects of modern urban conflict and to those who seek to better understand the military capabilities, strategy, and tactics of the Russian Federation.

For more information on RAND Arroyo Center, contact the Director of Operations (tel 310-393-0411, extension 6500; FAX 310-451-6952; e-mail donnab@rand.org), or visit the Arroyo Center's Web site at http://www.rand.org/organization/ard/.

CONTENTS

FIGURES

The Russian soldiers who entered the Chechen capital city of Grozny in December 1994 did not expect a fight. They were confident that their enemy, a rebel force seeking independence for Chechnya from Russian rule, was untrained and unorganized; that the sight of tanks in the streets would be sufficient to make them back down. The Russian soldiers had no reason to think otherwise. Their commanding officers had told them there was nothing to worry about.

It did not take long for the Russians to realize how wrong they had been. For the young men who spent New Year's Eve attacking the city, Grozny—which in Russian means "terrible" or "menacing"— lived up to its name. Although the Russians eventually managed to take control of the city, the learning curve was steep, and the costs high. Moreover, the victory was short-lived. A rebel counter-offensive followed by a negotiated settlement ended the war in Chechnya in the fall of 1996. Russian forces left the region.

They returned five years later for a replay. In December 1999 Russian troops again entered Grozny. As they had five years before, they proved unprepared for the strength and competence of their enemy, this time despite significant preparation and effort. Whereas complacency had been at fault in 1994, a very different dynamic was in play in 1999. If before the Russians had thought that a bloody urban battle was not a real danger, this time their military leaders believed they had a plan for avoiding such a necessity: artillery and air strikes, they thought, would force the enemy into submission. This plan justified the almost complete lack of attention to urban combat in preparatory training.

The Chechen resistance was prepared, however. Rather than being forced out by the Russians' artillery and air strikes, the rebels dug in and waited them out, taking advantage of a network of underground tunnels and bunkers. Then, when the Russian forces made their way in, their plans for subduing residual resistance proved to be insufficient, as they had a full-fledged defense on their hands. Because Russian troops had once again not been trained for the urban environment, they were again not prepared for the fight they faced.

If failure to prepare for urban combat was a key error the Russians made in both Chechnya wars, it was far from the only one. Hampered by poor training and supplies, decrepit equipment, and abysmal planning, the 1994–1996 war presented a stark picture of how much this once-great force had deteriorated. It also demonstrated how poorly Russian military organizational structures functioned when disparate forces were called upon to work together. The second war, which began in the fall of 1999 and continues today, shows some real improvements, particularly in planning, force coordination, basic tactics, and public relations. However, other difficulties remain.

Grozny I: Russian Errors

Deterioration

- Soldiers were untrained and many were unable to properly use night-vision equipment, armor, weaponry, etc. Moreover, much of the equipment was in poor condition, and military professionalism was sorely lacking in all ranks.

- Ad hoc units were assembled hastily and did not train together before they went into combat.

Unwarranted optimism

- Despite ample evidence to the contrary, the Russians believed the city was not well defended. They grossly underestimated their enemy and overestimated their own capabilities.

- Advance planning was haphazard, optimistic, and lacked contingency plans.

- The Russians did not conduct adequate intelligence preparation of the battlefield (IPB).

- Despite their commanders' claims to the contrary, Russian forces failed to seal all approaches to Grozny.

Problems of force coordination

- The wide range of ministries and organizations with troops deployed to Chechnya each had its own competing command structures.

- Coordination between Ministry of Defense (MoD) and Ministry of Internal Affairs (MVD) units, between ground and air forces, and among troops on the ground was abysmal.

- The myriad of forces failed to share intelligence with one another. They had incompatible communications equipment and protocols. Moreover, troops ignorant of their own protocols often communicated in the clear, risking their own lives and those of their comrades.

- Partly because of these problems, fratricide was a leading cause of death for Russian soldiers.

- There was little effort to pass lessons learned and tactics developed on to other soldiers. Hence, this hard-won knowledge was generally lost between one battle and the next.

Although this list was drawn predominantly from the Russian urban combat experience in Grozny, none of these mistakes is unique to the urban environment. Even the failure to recognize that urban terrain favors the defense is more broadly applicable (most terrain favors the defense). The problems the Russians faced in Grozny plagued them throughout the first Chechnya war.

Grozny II: Russian Improvements

The Russians carefully studied the mistakes of the first war, and their forces were able to make key improvements in a number of areas. Although little of the effort was geared to urban combat, the impact was nonetheless felt in the 1999–2000 battle for Grozny.

Preparation

- A thought-out plan, albeit one for subduing small pockets of resistance in a defeated city rather than attacking a defended metropolis, governed troop movements and limited confusion.

- A better, if still incomplete, seal of the city was effected.

- Improved food and supply provisions kept soldiers from starving on the front lines as they had in the last war.

- Strict control of the press and information, along with a professional public relations campaign, built and maintained public support.

Coordination

- A single hierarchy under MoD command simplified and improved command and control.

- Force coordination and synchronization of air and land operations improved vastly.

- Better IPB and information sharing made better planning and implementation possible.

Tactics

- Use of armor was safer and more effective.

- Use of standoff air and artillery attacks rather than going in for the close fight did not always work, but it may have saved the lives of a few soldiers.

- Slow and careful movement took the place of a haphazard and hazardous attempt to advance immediately to the city center.

- Forces closed to prompt a reaction, then immediately backed off to standoff range.

- Russia's few trained snipers were judiciously deployed and used.

- Massed firepower was used in lieu of manpower. This limited military casualties, but at a cost in infrastructure and noncombatants.

- Assault groups, increased authority to junior officers, and smaller units increased effectiveness and survivability.

- Increased use of specialized units to backstop the mostly conscript motorized rifle troops improved effectiveness and decreased casualties and fratricide.

Grozny II: Russian Errors

The key mistake the Russian military made between the wars was in drawing the wrong lesson from urban combat: not only that it should be avoided, but that it *could* be avoided, under all circumstances. They were therefore unprepared for it when it came. Moreover, many structural and organizational failings remained from the first war.

Failure to prepare for urban combat

- The Russians expected artillery and air strikes to lead to a decisive victory and had no contingency plans.

- Russian soldiers were not trained for urban combat and once again had to learn on the fly.

Deterioration and organizational failings

- The improved force coordination often broke down, leading to problems and recriminations particularly among MoD forces, MVD forces, and Chechen loyalist forces.

- The motorized rifle troops were still poorly trained.

- Equipment, particularly aircraft, was old and spare parts were lacking.

- Most Russian forces could not fight effectively at night.

Chechen Advantages

Of course, Russian failings were exacerbated by Chechen advantages. These were largely common to both wars' urban (and nonurban) combat. There is little reason to change an effective approach.

- The Chechens knew their cities and prepared to defend them.

- Many of the rebels had served in the Soviet and Russian armies. They made good use of Soviet MOUT lessons derived from the World War II experience.

- The rebels were able to maximize the advantages that accrue to the defense in urban terrain.

- Chechen small-unit organizing principles were ideal for urban terrain.

- "Hugging" rather than flanking tactics made it easier to exploit Russian weaknesses.

- Snipers were well-employed.

- A professional media campaign effectively manipulated global public opinion in 1994–1996 (but not 1999–2000).

- Their combat goal was less to "win" territory than to make staying in Chechnya unbearable for their opponent.

At the time of this writing, the Chechen war continues. It seems probable that, given time and determination, the Russians can "succeed" in Chechnya. But key to such success is their preponderance of manpower and firepower. Thus, they must choose between destroying the region, settling in for an extended and bloody occupation, or some equally unpleasant combination of the two. The Chechens are counting on them to decide that Chechnya is not worth the cost.

The Russian experience with urban combat in Chechnya is important for two reasons. First, the Chechnya wars and their urban component provide a unique opportunity to study Russia's military forces. The Russian combat experience can tell the careful observer a great deal about Russian capabilities, tactics, and capacity to learn from experience. The focus on urban combat does not preclude a broader understanding of Russian military planning and implementation. Rather, it focuses the analysis on a specific mission of interest while gleaning a range of widely applicable lessons.

Second, the Russian experience provides insight into the mechanics of urban combat. In an increasingly urbanized world, it is likely that soldiers will find themselves fighting repeatedly in cities, towns, and villages, where combatants can be difficult to distinguish from noncombatants. Thus, other militaries would be well-served to study the Russian experience.

There is excellent reason to believe that future enemies of the United States will look more like the Chechens than the Russians. Therefore, it behooves the United States to prepare for urban combat. As the Russians have learned, avoiding it, although preferable, is often impossible. U.S. planners should also recognize that a resident insurgency force enjoys significant advantages over even a technically superior foreign aggressor. It is better to learn from the experiences of others than to repeat their mistakes. The United States and its military forces should learn from the Russian experience.

ACKNOWLEDGMENTS

The author would like to thank Russell Glenn and Brian Nichiporuk, who headed an earlier project that led me to examine Russian writings on urban combat and Chechnya. Russell Glenn deserves additional thanks for encouraging the expansion of that exploration into the present effort. A debt of gratitude is also owed to Pamela Beatrice of the Office of the Deputy Assistant Secretary of the Army for Research and Technology and Eric Kraemer of the Office of the Deputy Chief of Staff for Intelligence, U.S. Army, under whose auspices this work was undertaken. The insightful advice and commentary of Lester Grau and Benjamin Lambeth greatly improved the quality of this analysis, and I am extremely grateful for their time and efforts. Special thanks are also due to Timothy Thomas and Kenneth Webb, who read and commented on earlier drafts. David Kassing and Thomas Szayna provided many helpful comments as the document was finalized, and I greatly appreciate their time and assistance. Finally, my assistant, Joanna Alberdeston, was crucial to the preparation of this manuscript, as was Nikki Shacklett, whose editing skills greatly enhanced its narrative flow. In thanking all of them, I emphasize that none of them are in any way to blame for any errors or oversights: those are mine alone.

A-50	Medium/long-range cargo/transport aircraft used to carry airborne warning and control system. NATO designation: Il-76 "Mainstay."
AGS-17	*Plamya.* 30mm automatic grenade launcher.
Alpha	Russian elite special forces unit.
AMPS	Acronym: Advanced Mobile Phone Service. Cellular telephone compatibility standard.
An-2	Light utility transport biplane that can operate from unimproved airfields and from water surfaces. Has stealth-like capabilities when flown at low speed and low altitude. NATO designation: "Colt."
An-26	Short-haul transport aircraft. NATO designation: "Curl."
An-30B	Aerial survey aircraft with same basic configuration as the An-26. NATO designation: "Clank."
APC	Acronym: Armored Personnel Carrier. Russian equivalent: BTR.
Arbalet-M	Russian radar system.
ATGM	Acronym: Anti-Tank Guided Missile. Russian equivalent: PTUR.

BMP	Russian acronym. English translation: Armored infantry fighting vehicle. Unlike BTRs, BMPs are tracked.
BMP-1	BMP originally built in the 1960s. Armed with machine guns and a 73mm short-range gun.
BRDM-2	Armored reconnaissance vehicle model.
BTR	Russian acronym. English equivalent: APC.
BTR-70	Armored personnel carrier. Introduced in 1979.
BTR-80	Successor to the BTR-70 with a diesel engine (instead of twin gas engines) and easier troop entry and exit. Initially introduced in the mid-1980s.
Buratino (TOS-1)	Heavy 30-barrel thermobaric (fuel-air) weapon system mounted on a T-72 chassis.
DShK	12.7mm machine gun.
EW	Acronym: Electronic warfare.
FSB	Russian acronym. English translation: Federal Security Service. Russian successor to the Soviet KGB.
Grad (BM-21)	40-tube 122mm truck-mounted multiple rocket launcher system. NATO designation: M1964.
Igla (9K310)	Shoulder-fired SAM. NATO designation: SA-16 "Gimlet."
Il-20	Reconnaissance EW aircraft. NATO designation: "Coot-A."
INMARSAT	Global mobile satellite system that provides communications services including a satellite telephone system.
Iridium	Global mobile satellite system that provides communications services including a satellite telephone system.

Ka-40	Anti-submarine warfare and transport/rescue helicopter. 24-hour, adverse weather–capable.
Ka-50	Close support/assault helicopter. Can operate at night if specially equipped. Often called "Black Shark." Also called "Werewolf" in the West. NATO designation: "Hokum."
KAB-500	Steerable air bomb with a 380-kg warhead. Can be equipped with either a laser or television guidance.
KAB-1500 L	Heavy laser-guided bomb with 1,180-kg warhead.
KAB-1500 TK	Heavy bomb with TV sights and 1,180-kg warhead.
KGB	Russian acronym. English translation: Committee for State Security. Soviet precursor to the FSB.
Kh-25 ML	Air-to-surface missile with laser spot seeker. NATO designation: AS-10.
KPVT	14.5mm heavy machine gun.
Krasnopol	22-km range, 152mm laser-designated artillery round.
MBT	Acronym: Main Battle Tank.
Mi-8	Transport helicopter. Also used for search and rescue. Has gunship and EW versions. NATO designation: "Hip."
Mi-24	Multimission assault helicopter. Used in fire support, escort, and anti-tank roles and in air-to-air combat against enemy helicopters. NATO designation: "Hind."
Mi-24N	Night vision–capable Mi-24.
MiG-25RB	Reconnaissance-bomber version of the MiG-25 fighter. NATO designation for the MiG-25: "Foxbat."
MiG-31	Fighter-interceptor. Follow-on to the MiG-25. NATO designation: "Foxhound."

MoD	Acronym: Ministry of Defense.
MOUT	Acronym: Military Operations in Urban Terrain.
Msta (2A65)	Large 152mm gun on a self-propelled howitzer system. NATO designation: M1986. The *Msta*-S (2S19) uses the same weapon as a self-propelled gun.
Mukha	RPG-18.
MVD	Russian acronym. English translation: Ministry of Internal Affairs.
NBC	Acronym: Nuclear/Biological/Chemical (equipment, troops, etc.).
NCO	Acronym: Noncommissioned Officer.
NMT-450	Analog cellular telephone network.
Nona	The *Nona*-K (2B16) is a 120mm towed gun/mortar system. The *Nona*-S (2S9) is a self-propelled version.
OMON	MVD special forces units with riot control and anti-terrorist training.
Pchela 1T	Remotely piloted reconnaissance UAV provides television surveillance of ground targets. Night-capable.
PK	Kalashnikov machine gun.
PTUR	Russian acronym. English equivalent: ATGM (Anti-Tank Guided Missile).
R-300 (8K14)	Mobile short-range ballistic missile for battlefield support. NATO designation: SS-1C "Scud-B."
RPG	Rocket-propelled anti-tank grenade launcher.
RPG-7	Standard man-portable short-range anti-tank weapon of former Warsaw Pact states, their allies, and their customers.

RPG-18	*Mukha*. Light anti-armor weapon. Small rocket with a motor that ignites on launch. The warhead is a 64mm shaped charge.
SA-7	*Strela*-2. Man-portable short-range shoulder-fired SAM. NATO designation: "Grail."
SA-14	See *Strela*-3.
SA-19	Anti-aircraft missile. NATO designation: "Grison."
SAM	Acronym: Surface-to-air missile.
Shilka	See ZSU 23-4.
Shmel (RPO-A)	New generation "flamethrower." 11-kg, single-shot, disposable, 600-meter range weapon carried in packs of two by ground forces. The warhead is equipped with a "thermobaric" incendiary mixture, a fuel-air explosive, which upon detonation produces an effect comparable to that of a 152mm artillery round.
SOBR	MVD special forces units with riot control and anti-terrorist training.
Spetsnaz	Russian special forces units. *Spetsnaz* is short for "spetzialnogo naznacheniya" or "special designation."
Stinger (FIM-92)	Light-weight, short-range, heat-seeking, man-portable SAM. U.S. design and production.
Strela-3 (9K34)	Improved version of the SA-7 with a more powerful motor and cryogenically cooled passive infrared homing seeker with proportional guidance. NATO designation: SA-14 "Gremlin."
Stroi-P system	UAV system equipped with a launching vehicle, command and control center, and 10 *Pchela*-1Ts.
Su-24	High-speed long-range strike aircraft capable of night and inclement weather operations. NATO designation: "Fencer."

Su-24M	Attack version of the Su-24. NATO designation: "Fencer-D."
Su-24MR	Reconnaissance variant of the Su-24 retains missile launch capability but no laser and TV sighting system or cannon. NATO designation: "Fencer-E."
Su-25	Subsonic close air support aircraft designed for use from unimproved airfields. NATO designation: "Frogfoot."
Su-27	Multirole fighter aircraft, also ground-attack capable. NATO designation: "Flanker."
SVD	7.62mm Dragunov sniper rifle.
T-62	MBT originally designed in 1962 with various improvements since then.
T-72	MBT originally designed in 1973 with numerous improvements since then.
T-80	MBT originally designed in 1976. Thought to be the principal tank in production for the Russian army.
T-80U	New version of T-80 with improved armor protection, updated 125mm gun, and a new fire control system.
Tochka	Single-warhead mobile short-range missile. NATO designation: SS-21 "Scarab."
Tochka-U	Improved version of the *Tochka*.
Tu-22M-3	Long-range high-performance medium bomber.
UAV	Acronym: Unmanned aerial vehicle.
UAZ	Civilian all-terrain vehicle similar to a Jeep.
Uragan (BM-22)	Multiple rocket launcher system. NATO designation: M1977.
VSS	9.3mm rifle.

ZPU-2	14.5mm anti-aircraft gun. Consists of two machine guns mounted on a two-wheel carriage. Precursor to the Zu-23. No longer in service with the Russian armed forces.
ZPU-4	14.5mm anti-aircraft gun. Consists of four machine guns mounted on a four-wheel carriage. Precursor to the Zu-23. No longer in service with the Russian armed forces.
ZSU	Russian acronym. Self-propelled anti-aircraft mount.
ZSU 23-4	*Shilka.* Air defense gun. Principal self-propelled anti-aircraft gun system in Russian ground forces.
ZSU-2S6	2S6 *Tungushka,* a gun/missile air defense vehicle armed with twin 30mm cannons and 8 SA-10 anti-aircraft missiles. The associated radar system is NATO designated "Hot Shot."
Zu-23	23mm twin-barrel towed anti-aircraft gun assigned to Russian airborne divisions.

Chapter One

INTRODUCTION

Кавказа гордые сыны,	Proud sons of the Caucasian mountains,
Сражались, гибли вы ужасно;	You fought and died so terribly;
Но не спасла вас наша кровь, . . .	But even our blood did not save you, . . .

From Alexander Pushkin,
Prisoner of the Caucasus, 1820–1821 (author's translation)

BACKGROUND

In December 1994, Russian troops embarked on a painful and bloody effort to wrest the city of Grozny, in the breakaway region of Chechnya, from secessionist forces. Despite expectations of easy victory, the city lived up to its name, which in Russian means "terrible" or "menacing." After taking numerous casualties and nearly destroying the city, the Russians eventually succeeded in capturing it. They then maintained control of Grozny for over a year, overcoming mul-

---

Author's note: In this analysis, I use the terms "rebel," "insurgent," "guerrilla," and "resistance" to refer to individuals and groups fighting the Russian forces with the goal of establishing and maintaining an independent Chechen state, the Republic of Ichkeria. These terms are not meant to connote any judgment on my part of the legitimacy or illegitimacy of any cause or action. Rather, I believe they conform to common usage for conveying that the individuals and groups referenced seek to secure independence from Russia. I also use the term "Chechen" to refer to these same individuals and groups. In doing so, I do not intend to imply that all individuals of Chechen descent, or all residents of the Chechen Republic, are involved in the effort to achieve independence from Russia. But because the effort was and is in most ways a Chechen nationalist one, I believe the use of the term is appropriate. When I refer to Chechen groups supporting Russian rule, I use modifiers such as "loyalist" to make that clear.

tiple Chechen attacks. But at the end of August 1996 an unexpected Chechen counteroffensive proved successful, and a subsequent negotiated settlement ended the Chechen conflict. Despite that agreement's commitment to joint rule, Russian forces soon left Grozny and Chechnya.

But this conflict had deep roots and it was far from over. Russians have fought to control the northern Caucasus region for centuries, battling the ancestors of those who live there now. The prize, then as now, was forested mountainous terrain that gives its defenders many advantages. Victory, when attained, has always been fleeting and costly. Moreover, throughout the centuries, each return of Russian forces fanned the flames of local hatred for Moscow's rule, spurring renewed rebellion. With this history in mind, it should come as no surprise that having left in August 1996, Russian soldiers returned to Grozny in December 1999 to once again battle Chechen rebels in the city's streets.

WIDER IMPLICATIONS OF THE CHECHEN WARS

This latest bout of fighting in Chechnya and its cities, towns, and villages has important implications for understanding and forecasting the future of war—and for U.S. military thinking and planning. However decrepit, undermanned, and undertrained the Russian military may be, it is the successor to the Soviet Army, and in some ways still the same force. For many years, Soviet military preparation, like that of the United States, focused almost exclusively on war in central Europe against a highly skilled, technologically advanced adversary. In Chechnya, Russia found many of these skills and capabilities to be incommensurate with fighting a comparatively low-technology enemy, especially in an urban environment where it repeatedly failed to anticipate the extent and capacity of enemy resistance. This is an important lesson, and not just for the Russians. The enemies that U.S. forces will face in the future are far more likely to resemble the Chechen rebels than the Russian Army, and the battlefield will very likely look more like Grozny than central Europe.

What happened to the Russians in Grozny and Chechnya's other towns and villages? Was the debacle of New Year's Eve 1994–1995 a result of military incompetence, or were the high casualties and ineffectual combat products of disadvantages inherent in fighting to capture, rather than defend, a city? Was the purported success of five years later a true victory, or a public relations whitewash of yet another slaughter? What does the sum of these battles for Grozny reveal about urban warfare specifically and Russian capabilities generally? What lessons can this experience teach the United States as it develops its own approaches to urban combat?

With these questions as a guide, this report explores the events of 1994–1996 and those of 1999–2000, comparing them and drawing lessons from both. While focusing primarily on urban combat, this analysis also discusses many general aspects of Russian operations in the Chechnya war. The conclusions it draws are neither clear nor easy ones, for there is truth to be found in a wide range of competing and sometimes incongruous-seeming explanations. All of them must be studied and understood. As one of the largest-scale urban operations of our time and a major test of the Russian armed forces, Grozny offers significant lessons to students of both the Russian military and urban combat.

APPROACH AND ORGANIZATION

This report provides a detailed look at the weapons and tactics employed during urban combat in Chechnya in 1994–1995 and 1999–2000, focusing primarily on the Russian experience. The analysis is informed by primary and secondary published and Internet sources and by interviews and discussions with military officers and other experts. This includes a comprehensive review of the Russian professional military press between 1995 and 2000 (*Armeiskii Sbornik*, *Voiennaia Mysl*, and others). Journalistic sources include Russian- and English-language media reports and press interviews with soldiers and officers on the front lines. Moreover, the research was informed by the already substantial literature on the Chechnya conflicts written by Russian and Western analysts.

The report is organized chronologically, with Chapter Two examining the 1994–1995 Chechnya campaign and Chapter Three focusing on the 1999–2000 campaign. Because there are already a number of authoritative analyses of the earlier campaign, Chapter Two relies more heavily on secondary sources. Rather than taking a detailed look at the campaign, the chapter summarizes the mistakes of and lessons learned by the Russian military. Chapter Three is more detailed in its description of the combat and relies more on primary source material. It discusses the major tactical aspects of urban combat and the innovations introduced by the Russians. Chapter Four provides overall conclusions regarding the preparation of the Russian armed forces for the type of urban combat they experienced in Chechnya, the extent of learning, and the potential lessons from the Russian experience applicable to other militaries.

Chapter Two

GROZNY I: 1994–1995

A STEP BACK: THE HISTORICAL CONTEXT

There is some truth to the argument that Russia's initial failures in Grozny and Chechnya as a whole can be traced directly to Moscow's reliance on out-of-date Soviet strategic thinking. The Soviets, expecting to fight in central and western Europe, believed that the enemy would prefer to declare its cities open rather than have them destroyed by combat. To the Soviets, therefore, urban terrain presented two options: if a city was defended, it was to be bypassed; if it was not, it could be taken from the march. In the latter case, entering troop formations would conduct a show of force rather than fight. Tanks would lead, followed by mounted and dismounted infantry.[1] The unwillingness to include serious urban combat in the Soviet concept of future war severely hampered Russia's ability to prepare for it.

Russia's entry into Grozny at the close of 1994 was conducted as just such a show of force, with tanks followed by mounted infantry. The Russians entered Grozny in this way because they believed that the city was not well defended. While this simple explanation is accurate, a more complex understanding of a far greater failure of Russian military thought provides more insight. The Russian approach to

---

[1]Lester W. Grau, *Changing Russian Urban Tactics: The Aftermath of the Battle for Grozny*, Fort Leavenworth, KS: Foreign Military Studies Office Publications, downloaded from *call.army.mil/call/fmso/fmsopubs/issues/grozny.htm.* Originally published as "Russian Urban Tactics: Lessons from the Battle for Grozny," *INSS Strategic Forum*, No. 38, July 1995.

Grozny, in both its conception and its implementation, provides damning evidence of the loss of (or disregard for) a tremendous body of knowledge. The Soviet Union had learned a great deal about urban fighting in World War II. It incorporated that knowledge into training and studies for subsequent generations of officers. Had all of this experience, all of this thought, somehow disappeared along with the Red Army?

The World War II German invasion found Soviet forces so unprepared for urban combat that they relied on scanty tactical writings from the 1920s to plan and orchestrate their defenses. Unsurprisingly, this approach had limited success. But as the war progressed the Red Army got better and better—first at urban defense, and later, as the tide turned, at the even more difficult task of offensive urban combat. That the Soviets learned from their mistakes is clear from the progression of the fighting, from the rapid loss of cities in the early days of the war to the successful defenses of Tula and Leningrad, the victory at Stalingrad, and successes in Budapest, Vienna, Konigsberg, and finally Berlin. Throughout the war, Soviet analysts recorded what worked and what did not, so that these lessons could be studied and understood long after the battles were over.[2]

This World War II experience became the basis of Soviet planning and training for urban terrain. One obvious lesson, despite early Soviet losses, was that urban warfare heavily favors the defense. Soviet tacticians argued that to capture and hold a city, the attacker requires an advantage of at least 4:1 (some said 6:1).[3] Another prerequisite for a successful attack on an urban area is an effective blockade (i.e., an encirclement of the city, sealing off all approaches) prior to the start of operations, combined with comprehensive intelligence and reconnaissance and detailed contingency planning.[4] Forces should enter the city in small teams prepared to fight hand-

---

[2]For a useful overview of World War II defensive tactics and the defensive lessons of that war, see G. P. Yefimov, "Features of the Defense of Large Cities and Industrial Areas," *Military Thought*, January 1, 1990.

[3]Grau, *Changing Russian Urban Tactics: The Aftermath of the Battle for Grozny*; Andrei Raevsky, "Chechnya: Russian Military Performance in Chechnya: An Initial Evaluation," *Journal of Slavic Military Studies*, December, 1995, p. 682.

[4]N. N. Novichkov et al., *The Russian armed forces in the Chechen conflict: analysis, results, conclusions* (in Russian), Paris, Moscow: Kholveg-Infoglob, Trivola, 1995, p. 64.

to-hand and house-to-house. Capture of buildings may be effected either by simultaneous attack from several directions or by crossing over from neighboring structures. Regardless of how the attack begins, the first step, once in the building, is to establish control over stairway landings, stairs, and upper floors using hand and smoke grenades. Once a building is captured it must be defended indefinitely to prevent its recapture by the enemy. Supply lines and flanks are susceptible to enemy counterattack. There, and elsewhere, consistent tank and artillery cover fire must protect infantry movements. Soviet scholars emphasized the importance of clear communications, especially as positions changed. Finally, Soviet analysts repeatedly noted the usefulness of the flamethrower. This weapon's particular effectiveness for clearing rooms and buildings made it a key tool in the Russian World War II urban warrior's arsenal.[5]

Red Army World War II forces also created special assault (or "storm") detachments and groups, specifically developed for independent action in urban terrain. Each detachment included a rifle battalion, a sapper company, an armor company or self-propelled assault gun battery, two mortar batteries, a cannon or howitzer battery, 1 or 2 batteries of divisional artillery, and a flamethrower platoon. The detachment was subdivided into 3 to 6 assault groups as well as a support group and a reserve. Each assault group, in essence a rifle company (the source says "platoon or company," but the structure described seems more appropriate to a company), included 1 or 2 sapper detachments, an anti-tank rifle detachment, 2 to 5 individually carried flamethrowers, smoke devices, 3 or 4 other man-portable weapons, and 2 or 3 tanks or self-propelled assault guns. If necessary, groups could be further subdivided to better focus specifically on such missions as fire, command, reserves, reconnaissance, and obstacle clearing. Individual soldiers were supplied with a large number of grenades and explosives. Training and preparation for the urban environment emphasized independent thought and action from each soldier and warned of the pitfalls of standardized procedure.[6]

---

[5]Ibid.

[6]Ibid.

Was all of this forgotten between the years of World War II and the post–Cold War battles in Grozny? To an extent, it was. During the late 1940s and early 1950s, Soviet analysts and soldiers diligently studied the urban fighting of the past, but as time went on, attention focused elsewhere. By the 1980s, urban combat was no longer the focus of in-depth exercises, and military textbooks ignored the issue almost entirely.[7] By 1994, neither the Ministry of Defense nor any of the other government organizations with troops at their command had any forces geared specifically to urban combat. The last such force was dissolved in February 1994, at which time 400 of its 430 officers retired.[8]

This is not to say that Russian forces were entirely untrained for operations in urban environments. The overall excellently prepared *Spetsnaz* (special forces units) and paratroopers continued to train for some urban contingencies.[9] The preparation of *Spetsnaz* and FSB[10] snipers, for instance, focused almost exclusively on urban situations. But with the end of the Cold War, the prognosis for urban deployments was that they would involve primarily small-scale counterterrorist actions, not full-blown warfare. Therefore, the special forces and others prepared for exactly this sort of contingency and Russian urban training sites supported such counterterrorism preparation, as well as perhaps some peacekeeping training. As a result, the motorized rifle troops that formed the bulk of the force in Grozny continued to prepare for the open-terrain warfare that was expected when the Cold War turned hot. Only five or six of the 151 total hours of squad, platoon, and company tactical training mandated by Russian training standards for forces bound for battle were dedicated to the urban environment. Moreover, the overall decline in actual training makes it unlikely that the troops that went into Grozny received even that preparation. For many, the sole preparation for the urban mission was an instructional pamphlet on urban combat prepared by the Main Combat Training Directorate of the

---

[7]Yefimov.

[8]Novichkov et al., pp. 67–68.

[9]*Spetsnaz* and paratroop forces are separate from the air force and ground forces in Russia.

[10]The Federal Security Service and the successor organization to the KGB. Like "KGB," the acronym "FSB" reflects the Russian terminology.

Ground Forces and printed in such small numbers that troops had to share. Even army snipers had little specialized training. National sniper schools were shut down in 1952 and "sniper" training became a regimental responsibility, often limited to simply selecting soldiers and officers who appeared to be good shots. Although specific sniper roles were laid out in training exercises and formations, actual training and preparation were minimal.[11]

INTO GROZNY

It is quite plausible that the Russian dictat to bypass defended cities was not a result of careful consideration but rather the only course available to a force that had stopped preparing for urban combat years before. Had the Russians believed Grozny to be well defended, then, they would almost certainly not have entered the city in 1994. Indeed, Russian commanders instructed their subordinates not to expect a fight.[12] Minister of Defense General Pavel Grachev probably expected minimal resistance—if not the experience of Prague in 1968, chastened dependents frightened into a stand-down by a show of force, then something only marginally more difficult.[13] Instead, the Chechens were ready and willing to defend Grozny, and the Russians found themselves in a fight they did not want, expect, or prepare for. This was less a fault of strategic concepts, however, than an egregious failure to conduct necessary intelligence and reconnaissance in advance and to recognize the lessons of Chechen loyalists' unsuccessful efforts to recapture the city in preceding months.

General Grachev personally briefed the plan for the capture of Grozny. It consisted of three stages: Stage I would begin on November 29, 1994 and be over by December 6 (eight days). Over the course of this week, forces would prepare and secure locations from which

---

[11]"Urban Warfare: Lessons from the Russian Experience in Chechnya 1994–1995," *http://www.geocities.com/Pentagon/6453/chechnyaA.html;* e-mail exchange with BG John Reppert (ret.), former U.S. Defense Attaché to Russia, December 10, 1999; Dmitri Litovkin, "Sniper signature," *Krasnaya Zvezda,* Internet edition, April 14, 2000.

[12]Gregory J. Celestan, *Wounded Bear: The Ongoing Russian Military Operation in Chechnya,* Fort Leavenworth, KS: Foreign Military Studies Office Publications, 1996, downloaded from *call.army.mil/call/fmso/fmsopubs/issues/wounded/wounded.htm.*

[13]E-mail exchange with BG John Reppert (ret.), December 10, 1999, based on General Reppert's personal conversations with General Grachev.

operations would later be conducted while forward aviation and attack helicopters attained air superiority and other units prepared for electronic warfare. Three days, December 7–9, were allocated for Stage II, during which Russian troops would approach Grozny from five directions and effect a double encirclement—of the city and of the republic as a whole—all the while protecting communications and carrying out reconnaissance. The next four days, December 10–14, would comprise Stage III: the actual assault on Grozny. Forces would move from the north and south of the city to capture the Presidential Palace and other key government buildings, television and radio facilities, and other significant sites.[14]

Grachev's ambitious timetable began slipping early. Although the Russian air force had little trouble eliminating Chechnya's 266 aircraft in late November, the mass of Russian troops did not begin to move until December 11. As they maneuvered through the North Caucasus, they met unexpected opposition from the local population. This slowed them down and forced revision of Grachev's schedule, for the troops were not in place around Grozny until December 26.[15] Even then, and in fact throughout the campaign, the city stayed relatively porous, especially in the south. The planned "seal" never materialized.[16] General-Colonel Leontiy Shevtsov claimed that this was done on purpose, to enable the evacuation of refugees. Whether or not this was true, the open approaches also enabled Chechen resistance fighters to move in and out of the city and ensure their forces' supply and reinforcement. Russia itself was a primary source of both rebel forces and supplies, which generally traveled to Chechnya by way of the Ingush Republic.[17]

---

[14]Novichkov et al., pp. 28–29; "Military lessons of the Chechen campaign: preparation for the beginning of military actions (December, 1994)" (in Russian), *Oborona i Bezopasnost'*, October 23, 1996; Vladimir Mukhin and Aleksandr Yavorskiy, "War was lost not by the army, but by politicians" (in Russian), *Nezavisimaya Gazeta—Osobaya Papka*, Internet edition, No. 37 (2099), February 29, 2000.

[15]Benjamin S. Lambeth, *Russia's Air Power at the Crossroads*, Santa Monica, CA: RAND, 1996, pp. 200–201; "Military lessons of the Chechen campaign: preparation for the beginning of military actions (December, 1994)"; Mukhin and Yavorskiy.

[16]Novichkov et al., p. 30.

[17]"Military lessons of the Chechen campaign: the Grozny operation" (in Russian), *Oborona i Bezopasnost'*, No. 133–134, November 11, 1996; Mukhin and Yavorskiy; Novichkov et al., p. 44.

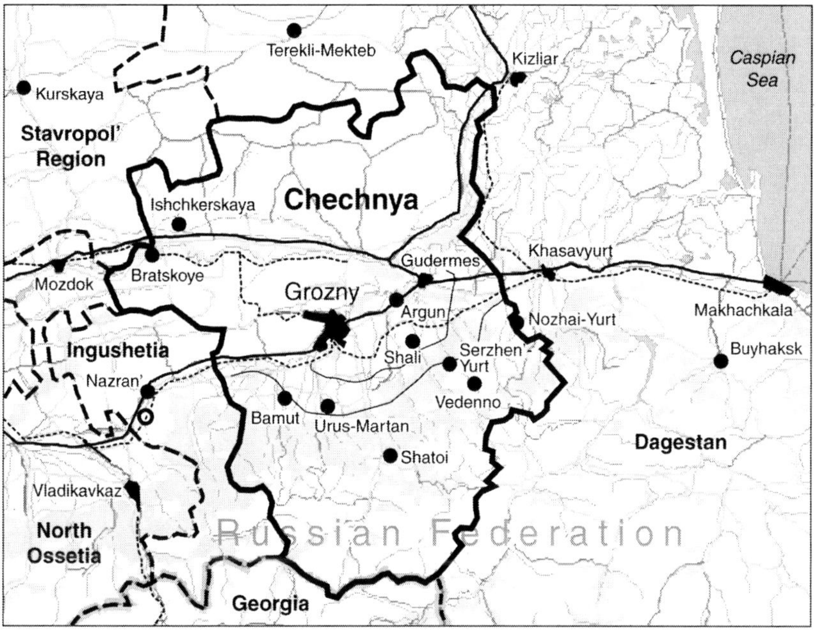

SOURCE: Anatoly S. Kulikov, "The First Battle of Grozny," in Russell W. Glenn (ed.), *Capital Preservation: Preparing for Urban Operations in the Twenty-First Century— Proceedings of the RAND Arroyo-TRADOC-MCWL-OSD Urban Operations Conference March 22-23, 2000*, Santa Monica, CA: RAND, CF-162-A, 2001. Used with permission of General Kulikov.

Figure 1—Chechnya

Grachev's plan and timetable reflect expectations of limited resistance. Poor intelligence and faulty planning were to blame. Preparation was sloppy, with reconnaissance limited to passive reports of what could be easily observed. Maps were inadequate and of the wrong scale.[18] Intelligence gathering did not begin in earnest until after military operations were under way.[19] Furthermore, ground

---

[18]Novichkov et al.; Grau, *Changing Russian Urban Tactics.*

[19]"Military lessons of the Chechen campaign: the Grozny operation," op. cit., November 11, 1996.

force commanders were loath to utilize their own resources for this mission, relying instead on air power. This, in turn, was hampered by poor weather conditions.[20] But even in perfect weather, air assets are a suboptimal reconnaissance tool over an urban battlefield, where enemy preparations can take place out of sight, e.g., within buildings. Planning also largely disregarded the experience of loyalist Chechen forces (which included some Russian troops) that had attempted assaults on Grozny in August, October, and November of 1994. If that experience had been studied, the Russian command would have been aware of the dangers that faced tank columns in Grozny. Only a few weeks before, in November, loyalist Chechen tank formations were surrounded and destroyed by RPG-armed rebels in the city.[21]

It was in part because of these failures of reconnaissance and planning that the Russian troops who entered Grozny thought their mission involved nothing more than a show of force. Three armored columns in herringbone formations were to move toward the city center from their camps in the outskirts in the north, east, and west. Then, with the assistance of special forces from the Ministry of Internal Affairs (MVD) and FSB, they were to capture key buildings and seal off the central part of the city and the Katayama region. Forces moving from the north and northeast were responsible for taking control of the northern part of the city center and the Presidential Palace. The western force was to capture the railway station and then, moving north, seal off the palace from the south. To prevent enemy military operations in the south and to preclude enemy resupply, it was also to seal off the Zavod and Katayama regions. At the same time, forces from the east were to move along the rail line and capture the bridges over the Sunzha River. They would then link up with the northern and western forces and thus completely isolate the center of the city. This coordinated action was expected to effectively surround and isolate Chechen leader Djohar Dudaev's forces, assumed to be concentrated in the city center.[22]

---

[20]"Military lessons of the Chechen campaign: preparation for the beginning of military actions (December, 1994)," October 23, 1996. See also Lambeth.

[21]"How it was taken" (in Russian), *Vremya Moscow News*, February 7, 2000.

[22]Novichkov et al., p. 46; Grau, *Changing Russian Urban Tactics: The Aftermath of the Battle for Grozny*.

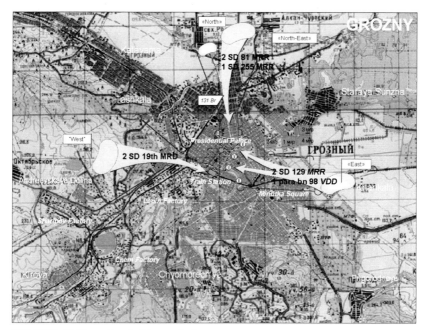

SOURCE: Kulikov. Used with permission.

Figure 2—Grozny: Plan of Attack, December 1994

All might have gone as planned if Russian expectations had proved correct. But instead of light resistance from a few small bands, the 6,000-man Russian force that attempted to penetrate the city on New Year's Eve found itself fighting an enemy far better prepared for battle and much larger than expected (estimates vary widely, from a low of about 1,000 to a high of ten times that amount). Moreover, the Chechens enjoyed the advantages of defense in an urban environment, while the Russians were faced with the far more difficult offensive task. Within the first hours of battle, Russian units were trapped in the streets, their armored vehicles destroyed by enemy troops shooting from upper and lower stories of buildings that main tank guns could not effectively engage. As had happened fifty years before in Berlin, entire tank columns were effectively paralyzed by the immobilization of the lead and trail vehicles.[23] Russian infantry troops unwittingly collaborated in their destruction by remaining within their APCs, mistakenly believing they were safer inside the armored vehicles than out. Russian soldiers fell by the hundreds.[24]

If a lack of preparation and reconnaissance had brought the Russian troops into central Grozny in the first place, a wide array of additional factors made up the debacle of how they fought once they got there. The force that moved on Grozny was not adequately trained or prepared for the urban battlefield or for any other. Composed of conscripts and haphazardly assembled ad hoc units, few of its soldiers had trained together before they were sent into Grozny's streets. But an individual lack of experience among young conscripts was not the only problem. Older contract soldiers who had signed up voluntarily did not do much better.[25] The Russian army was simply in no shape to fight a war. It had not held a divisional or regimental field exercise since 1992. It suffered tremendous shortages of junior officers and qualified NCOs.[26] The military was receiving perhaps 30–40 percent of its requirements for funding and supplies, and not a single regiment was at full strength.[27]

Another key problem was coordination. The troops deployed to Chechnya reported to a number of different ministries and organizations (Ministry of Defense, MVD, Federal Security Bureau, etc.) and included air, ground, paratroop, and *Spetsnaz* forces. These ministries and organizations had little experience working together, and their efforts to do so were often ineffectual. MVD forces could not coordinate with air and heavy armor forces or vice versa. The plethora of commanders that each group insisted on sending complicated decisionmaking and planning. Because communications procedures and equipment were often incompatible, intelligence frequently could not be shared, and units were unable to transmit their locations to supporting air forces. Such difficulties hampered

---

[23]Grau, *Changing Russian Urban Tactics: The Aftermath of the Battle for Grozny.*

[24]Mukhin and Yavorskiy.

[25]Ibid.

[26]"Special Report, The Chechen Conflict: No End of a Lesson?" *Jane's Intelligence Review,* September 1, 1996.

[27]Mukhin and Yavorskiy.

operations and increased tension, particularly between the Ministry of Defense and MVD troops. This was exacerbated as fighting continued and MoD troops accused their MVD counterparts of lagging behind when entering the more dangerous areas in Grozny.[28]

Even unhampered by their colleagues, the various units and groups deployed had their share of problems. Some of these were imposed from above. Russian units on the ground were hampered by impractical rules of engagement forbidding fire unless the enemy had shot first.[29] Fixed-wing aircraft were blocked from providing support for the New Year's Eve attack on the city by a December 24 presidential order prohibiting bombing of Grozny. Although Russian air assets had flown bombing missions over Chechnya and Grozny in November and December, among other things destroying the Chechen 266-plane air force on the ground, Su-25 and Su-24 planes did not support the ground attack on the city until January 3.[30]

When air assets did join the battle, their efforts were significantly constrained by poor weather. Russian forces therefore relied heavily on Su-24M attack aircraft, which are capable of operating in adverse weather conditions and at night. Flying at an altitude of 4,000–5,000 meters, the Su-24M generally carried 500-kg bombs with laser and TV guidance systems and Kh-25 ML (AS-10) missiles. The 1,500-kg laser-guided bombs were used less frequently, and a variety of standard munitions were also dropped on the city. In addition, MiG-31s and Su-27s flew patrols to prevent any Chechen air resupply. But the dominant role played by attack aircraft in Grozny was the destruction of bridges, buildings, and other structures designated by ground forces. Predictably these missions were often affected by communication failures and the fog of war, with some disastrous results.[31] On more than one occasion, aircraft targeted Russian troops instead of

---

[28]Novichkov et al., p. 25; "Military lessons of the Chechen campaign: the Grozny operation."

[29]Novichkov et al., p. 26.

[30]Aleksandr Yavorskiy, "Pilots not given time to turn around" (in Russian), *Nezavisimoye Voyennoye Obozreniye*, December 10, 1999; Lambeth, pp. 200–203.

[31]Ibid.

the adversary. In one instance, aircraft destroyed the five lead vehicles of the 104th Russian Airborne Division.[32]

Aviation was not alone in causing fratricide. Poor training and the lack of coordination also contributed to a significant number of such incidents. One participant estimated that fratricide accounted for as much as 60 percent of Russian casualties in Chechnya.[33] Russian motorized rifle troops were particularly in danger of both inflicting and becoming "friendly" casualties. Untrained troops who panicked and shot wildly at anything that moved were at least as likely to hit a fellow Russian as they were the enemy. Night-vision equipment proved ineffective in the smoke, fire, and steam of the city and led to accidental attacks on friendly forces. Inaccurate maps added further to the confusion. Poor use of equipment also helped the enemy. Russian infrared night-vision devices highlighted their users when viewed through the passive night-vision goggles used by the rebels.[34]

IN GROZNY: CHECHEN STRATEGY AND TACTICS

The Russians' lack of advance planning placed them in stark contrast to their adversary. According to Russian sources, Chechens had been preparing for the battle of Grozny for at least 3–4 months before Russian troops entered the city. During this time they developed war plans, divided up zones of responsibility, trained their militia, and set up effective communications.[35] In fact, they were putting into practice all the things that Soviet analysts had identified as key lessons of World War II.[36] Russian press descriptions of the rebel force as a set of loose groupings of bandits were inaccurate. The rebels were well-trained and drilled, many of them veterans of the

---

[32]Novichkov et al.

[33]Ibid., p. 70, citing an unnamed counterintelligence officer quoted in an *Izvestia* article of February 15, 1995.

[34]Vasiliy Geranin, "Terrible lessons of Grozny" (in Russian), *Armeyskiy Sbornik*, May 1998, pp. 22–24; Timothy Jackson, *David Slays Goliath: A Chechen Perspective on the War in Chechnya (1994–1996)*, Appendix C, "Chechen Technique for Urban Ambushes," Marine Corps Warfighting Lab, 2000.

[35]Bakar Taysumov, "On the eve of a metropolitan clash" (in Russian), *Nezavisimaya Gazeta*, February 6, 1997.

[36]Yefimov.

Soviet military who had apparently retained more of their training than had many of their Russian counterparts. As fighting continued, the rebel force would prove itself an effective military organization, albeit one with a less hierarchical structure than typically found in state armies. Furthermore, the rebel soldiers knew their city well, and their relatively light weapons (automatic rifles, grenades, and portable anti-tank weapons) tremendously enhanced the mobility that was central to their tactics. Closely set buildings and a network of underground passages enabled them to change position unseen by the Russians. (There is some uncertainty as to whether or not the sewage tunnel system was used. Russian sources insist that it was; some Chechen sources argue otherwise.) In addition to small arms, the rebel arsenal included truck-mounted multibarrel *Grad* rocket launchers, a handful of T-72 and T-62 tanks, BTR-70s, some self-propelled assault guns as well as anti-tank cannon, and some portable anti-aircraft missiles (difficult-to-credit reports suggest that these included U.S.-manufactured Stingers). Ammunition included shaped charges.[37] While there were reports that Chechens improvised chlorine gas weapons from industrial chemicals, these are difficult to confirm. It is clear that the bulk of the weaponry at the rebels' disposal had been left in Chechnya or sold by departing Russian troops in 1992.[38] Some items had even been officially transferred to Chechen forces by the Russian army.[39] Of those Chechen militia members who were not veterans of the Soviet/Russian armed forces, a good number may have trained abroad, for instance in Azerbaijan, Pakistan, or Turkey.[40]

---

[37]It is possible, but not likely, that Stingers were brought by volunteers from other Islamic countries, such as Afghanistan, who assisted the Chechen cause. But Stingers would almost certainly have resulted in higher kill rates against Russian air assets than were demonstrated. It seems more plausible that the reports of Stingers were a Chechen deception effort against Russian air operations. Novichkov et al., p. 45; "Russian Military Assesses Errors of Chechnya Campaign," *Jane's International Defense Review*, April 1, 1995; Jackson.

[38]"Urban Warfare: Lessons from the Russian Experience in Chechnya 1994–1995."

[39]Viktor Loshak, "Second-rate people behind the wheel of the army" (in Russian), *Moskovskiye Novosti*, No. 9 (1026), Internet edition, March 7–13, 2000, *http://www.mn.ru/2000/09/71.html*.

[40]Pavel Fel'gengauer, "Generals should not be berated, but rather retrained" (in Russian), *Segodnya*, December 25, 1996.

According to Russian sources, the Chechens were not concentrated entirely in the center of the city as the Russian forces had thought. Rather, they were distributed over three separate circles of defense. The inner circle was formed at a radius of 1–1.5 kilometers around the Presidential Palace. Its task was to use the buildings around the palace to mount a defense. The lower and upper floors of these buildings were modified to enable rifle and anti-tank weapon fire. Along the roads leading into the city center, positions were established to support direct artillery and tank fire. The center circle extended outward an additional kilometer in the northwest, and up to 5 kilometers to the southwest and southeast. These forces created strongpoints on bridges over the river, along relevant streets, and in the Minutka Square region. They were also prepared to blow up the chemical factory and oil industry infrastructure in the city. Finally, the outer circle followed the perimeter of the city and included populated points on its outskirts.[41]

It should be noted that the above description of Chechen defenses reflects a Russian perspective, and many Chechen sources underplay the degree of advance preparation, the scope of defenses, and their own numbers. They argue, somewhat incongruously, both that the Russians were in even worse shape than they appeared and that the resistance was able to overcome great numerical and technological odds not so much through planning and tactics as through ideological righteousness and tenacity. Regardless of the exact degree of Chechen defensive planning, there is no doubt that the rebels were better prepared than the Russians expected.

Reportedly, the Chechen resistance had managed to obtain the Russian attack plans, granting them a significant advantage. They also had access to Russian communications, which in the early days of conflict were transmitted in the clear, in large part because the forces operating the equipment were not familiar with the necessary procedures for secure communications. While one should view with skepticism reports of Chechen use of cellular telephones, given the absence of a cellular network in the region at the time, the rebels did possess Russian radios as well as hand-held Motorola radios, and

---

[41]Novichkov et al., p. 50; "Military lessons of the Chechen campaign: the Grozny operation."

were thus well equipped to both communicate with each other and overhear Russian transmissions. Furthermore, they were able to transmit disinformation over Russian radio channels to draw Russian forces into harm's way. Rebel gunmen also hampered Russian communications by targeting personnel carrying radios, thus successfully eliminating a large number of radio telephone operators. For their own communications, hand-held Motorola and Nokia radios were sufficient, and simply speaking in their native language was enough to keep communications secure given the dearth of Chechen-speaking Russians.[42] The Chechens' security was also enhanced by careful control of information, which was disseminated strictly on a need-to-know basis.[43]

Russian and Chechen sources agree that nonstandard squads were the basis of the rebel force. Such a squad might include two men with RPG-7 or *Mukha* (RPG-18) shoulder-fired anti-tank grenade launchers, two with machine guns, and possibly a sniper. Alternatively, it could comprise one man with a machine gun, one with an RPG, and possibly a sniper, backed up by one or more riflemen, automatic riflemen, ammunition bearers, and/or medics/corpsmen. Approximately three such squads, with support, made up a larger 25-man cell. The support included one or more medics/corpsmen, three ammunition/supply personnel, three litter bearers, and two SVD-armed snipers. Three 25-man groups made up a 75-man unit. Each of the latter was also allocated one mortar crew.[44]

This structure contributed significantly to the effectiveness of resistance ambushes. The rebels divided the city into quadrants (the city's managers and planners had been involved in developing its defense). Within those quadrants, 75-man units deployed along parallel streets with the snipers in covering positions. One 25-man subgroup, which included the unit command, deployed in smaller, six- or seven-man formations in the lower stories of buildings along one side of a street (to avoid crossfire and to establish escape routes).

---

[42]Timothy Thomas, *The Battle of Grozny: Deadly Classroom for Urban Combat*, Fort Leavenworth, KS: Foreign Military Studies Office Publications, downloaded from *call.army.mil/call/fmso/fmsopubs/issues/battle.htm* (first appeared in *Parameters*, Summer 1999, pp. 87–102); Mukhin and Yavorkskiy; Jackson.

[43]Jackson.

[44]Ibid.

The other two 25-man teams deployed similarly in basements and lower stories at the point of entry to the ambush site. From there they could seal off the area and reinforce their compatriots, as needed. In some cases, they also mined the buildings at the point of entry. As Russian forces approached, the entry-point teams notified the rest of the unit by Motorola radio—one for each six- or seven-man formation. Then, the command gave the order to seal the street and the attack began.[45]

Rather than "flanking" Russian forces in the traditional sense of the term, the guerrillas looked for weak points to attack. "Hugging" the Russian forces as they moved, the rebels were able to set up firing positions from 50 to 250 meters away and remain safe from artillery and rocket strikes.[46] Positions in the basements kept the rebels safe from Russian tank guns, the turrets of which were unable to depress their tubes sufficiently. Inexperienced Russian gunners were confused by simultaneous attacks by multiple Chechen teams. Not only did they not know where to shoot, with so many targets, but many of them were unable to target and fire while the vehicle was moving. Moreover, the rebels had reinforced the basements and subbasements from which they fought, turning them into bunkers. Vaulted and sloped add-on roofs reduced the effects of Russian RPO-A *Shmel* flamethrower and other systems.

Thus, as the Russians entered an ambush, resistance snipers and machine gunners could eliminate supporting infantry while anti-tank forces took out the armored vehicles. Chechen familiarity with Russian equipment was a key advantage as they successfully targeted the fuel cells and engines of armored vehicles, effecting kills with a minimum of rounds (an average of 3–6 lethal hits to destroy each tank). Their odds may have been improved by modifications to the RPG-7 that increased its explosive capacity and thus its ability to penetrate tank armor. Knowing to avoid the reactive armor at the front of many of the Russian tanks (which a number of the T-72s and T-80s went into battle without), the rebels focused their fire on the top, rear, and sides. They also knew how to attack vulnerable APCs such as the BMP-1. In addition to RPG rounds, gasoline and jellied

---

[45]Kulikov; Jackson.

[46]Ibid.

fuel were reportedly dropped onto the Russian vehicles and ignited. The Russians helped the matter along by remaining in tank columns, which, as already noted, could be trapped by immobilizing the first and last vehicles. Rebels in position within buildings along the street could then destroy the column methodically with their RPGs. The use of multiple teams helped overcome the problems presented by the RPG's signature backblast and the time required between shots.[47]

Chechen snipers, whether operating alone or as part of an ambush group, nightly terrified Russian soldiers, who dubbed them "ghosts." They were no less deadly in daylight.[48] A common sniper ploy was to shoot individual soldiers in the legs. When others tried to help the wounded soldiers, they too came under fire. But snipers were not alone in employing "dirty tricks" against the Russians. Resistance fighters booby-trapped the bodies of dead Russian soldiers and the entryways to buildings, the latter with strings of grenades and TNT. (It should be noted that some Chechen sources claim they made no use of booby-traps or mines within buildings because they feared the possibility of friendly casualties.) Chechen fighters sometimes disguised themselves as Red Cross workers, donning the identifying armbands. They also passed themselves off as civilians and offered to guide Russian forces through the city, instead leading them into ambushes.[49]

Mobility also contributed to rebel successes. Mortar crews remained on the move almost constantly. Having fired three or four rounds, they would quickly drive away from the area to preclude effective counterbattery fire. Troops armed with anti-tank rocket launchers reportedly traveled through the city in automobiles with the roofs

---

[47]Novichkov et al., p. 43; Lester W. Grau, *Russian-Manufactured Armored Vehicle Vulnerability in Urban Combat: The Chechnya Experience*, Fort Leavenworth, KS: Foreign Military Studies Office Publications, downloaded from *call.army.mil/ call/fmso/fmsopubs/ issues/rusav/rusav.html* (originally appeared in *Red Thrust Star*, January 1997); Jackson.

[48]Jackson.

[49]Ibid.; Novichkov et al., pp. 43–45; Thomas, *The Caucasus Conflict and Russian Security: The Russian Armed Forces Confront Chechnya III. The Battle for Grozny 1–26 January 1995*, Fort Leavenworth, KS: Foreign Military Studies Office Publications, downloaded from *call.army.mil/call/fmso/fmsopubs/issues/chechpt3.htm* (first appeared in *Journal of Slavic Military Studies*, Vol. 10, No. 1, March 1997, pp. 50–108); Thomas, *The Battle of Grozny: Deadly Classroom for Urban Combat*.

and backseats removed, perhaps to provide more room for men and equipment. In addition to heavy machine guns, the Chechens had some number of portable SA-7s and SA-14s for use against Russian air assets. In mountain towns, although not in Grozny, anti-air guns such as the ZPU-2 and ZPU-4 were mounted on truck beds. This weaponry was reportedly reasonably successful at bringing down Russian helicopters despite countermeasures (chaff and flares) that decreased SA-7 effectiveness.[50]

The Chechens also took steps to influence public opinion. The large number of journalists in the area had virtually unlimited access to Grozny, as Moscow made little effort to constrain their movements. The rebels were very open to press interest, granting interviews and generally making themselves available to domestic and foreign journalists. But they were also not averse to more creative approaches. For instance, the few tanks the rebels had were dug into multistory buildings in the center of the city. When the Chechens fired from these positions, Russian return fire inevitably hit civilian housing, schools, hospitals, and day care centers. When the cameras recorded and sent these images home, the Russians looked especially heartless, and the Chechens appeared even more the victims.[51]

LEARNING UNDER FIRE: THE EVOLUTION OF RUSSIAN TACTICS

Because the Chechens had a trained force, better tactics, and the advantages of the defense, they were initially able to defeat the poorly trained, undermanned Russian force that sought to capture Grozny without an effective plan. But that the Russians were able to stage a comeback, albeit with much loss of life and equipment, is a testament to the ability of soldiers to learn and adapt under fire. Key to the turnaround was leadership, albeit leadership developed and identified by survival of the fittest.[52] Shortly after the first days' debacle, Generals Nikolai Staskov and V. Petruk, commanders of the

---

[50]Novichkov et al., pp. 43–44; Jackson.

[51]Novichkov et al., pp. 43–45; Thomas, *The Caucasus Conflict and Russian Security: The Russian Armed Forces Confront Chechnya III. The Battle for Grozny 1–26 January 1995*; Thomas, *The Battle of Grozny: Deadly Classroom for Urban Combat.*

[52]Fel'gengauer.

committed airborne forces and 19th Motor Rifle Division, respectively, were relieved of their commands.[53] Russian forces were reorganized into three "Joint Groupings" with Generals Lev Rokhlin, Ivan Babich, and Vladimir Popov in command.[54]

The new leadership had a different, more systematic approach that drew effectively on the lessons of the past. The late General Rokhlin reported that he had adapted his tactics in Grozny from World War II urban attacks, particularly in Berlin.[55] Reinforcements also helped the Russians rebound. Russian forces in Chechnya reached 30,000 by February 1995, with significant concentration near Grozny. This gave Russia a definitive numerical advantage over the rebels, although still less of one than World War II analysts believed was needed to capture a city. Furthermore, the reinforcements were, by and large, more experienced and capable than the troops who had fought the first battles. They included elite airborne and *Spetsnaz* troops as well as naval infantry who deployed as complete units—in contrast to the hastily assembled groups that had gone into battle on New Year's Eve.[56] Thanks to their training and additional equipment, Russian forces could now carry out night rescue, reconnaissance, and attack. The MVD and FSB deployed snipers to supplement the untrained MoD sniper-designees.[57] Russian troops even used remotely piloted reconnaissance vehicles for the first time in combat.[58] Communications improved with secure voice transmitters and careful use of communications equipment to prevent targeting by enemy forces.[59] Effective tactics were emulated and improved. For instance, some of the units that had been cut off during the initial fighting managed to capture and hold the area around the

---

[53]Thomas, *The Caucasus Conflict and Russian Security: The Russian Armed Forces Confront Chechnya III. The Battle for Grozny 1–26 January 1995.*

[54]Raevsky, p. 685, footnote 42.

[55]E-mail exchange with BG John Reppert (ret.), who cites personal conversations with General Rokhlin, December 10, 1999. General Reppert served as the United States Defense Attaché to Russia from 1995 to 1997 and as the Army Attaché previously.

[56]"Special Report, The Chechen Conflict: No End of a Lesson?"; Raevsky, p. 685; Mukhin and Yavorskiy.

[57]Litovkin.

[58]Novichkov et al., p. 44; Raevsky, pp. 685–686.

[59]Thomas, *The Battle of Grozny: Deadly Classroom for Urban Combat.*

train station, as well as some other key sites. The rest of the force studied and copied the actions that led to such successes, and Russian troops learned to methodically capture multistory buildings and defend them. They began to task organize forces into small mobile assault groups, made better use of snipers and heavy artillery, and made sure that units talked to each other and to air assets, so that mutual support was possible.[60]

Self-propelled anti-aircraft machine guns (ZSU 23-4 *Shilka* and 2S6) were included in armored columns. These weapons could reach the Chechen hunter-killer teams lurking above or below a tank's main gun elevation and depression limits. Improved artillery planning provided concentrated artillery fire when Russian positions were attacked.[61]   Russian forces used searchlights and pyrotechnics to identify forces and blind enemy night-vision equipment.[62] Although the January 2, 1995, Russian government claims that the center of the city was under federal control were premature, there had been progress.[63] By January 6, General Babichev's troops were moving steadily toward the center of the city, reinforced by GRU *Spetsnaz* reconnaissance specialists and supported by artillery. By January 8, the fighting was localized in the center of the city and Russian snipers and artillery had denied the enemy the use of bridges over the river. On January 19, Russian forces destroyed the Presidential Palace with high-explosive concrete-piercing bombs. If this action fell far short of ending the battle for Grozny (after all, the same thing could have been done much earlier), it did have a certain psychological impact and provided a morale boost for Russian troops.[64]

In the weeks that followed, Russian and rebel forces continued to scramble for position. But the Russians had learned from past mistakes. Perhaps most important, they no longer assumed that captured buildings or territory would remain under their control. Instead, each building had to be captured and defended individually, as in World War II. Russian tactics continued to evolve. New

---

[60]Novichkov et al., pp. 54–55.

[61]Ibid., pp. 53, 62.

[62]Grau, *Changing Russian Urban Tactics: The Aftermath of the Battle for Grozny.*

[63]"How it was taken."

[64]Novichkov et al., pp. 54–55.

workarounds and approaches, some fairly self-evident, others less so, were tested and adopted as fighting continued. They included the increased use of smoke screens, including ones created with white phosphorus. The white phosphorus also incapacitated enemy forces. Russian troops learned to carry portable ladders and grappling hooks and use them to enter buildings. Soldiers also began to toss grenades through windows and doors prior to entry. They used mortars, heavy weapons, and RPO-A *Shmel* flamethrowers to systematically eliminate enemy snipers and defensive positions. When attacking a building, small combat teams cleared each room separately. When preparing buildings for defense, the Russians booby-trapped and mined potential enemy positions and axes of attack, including underground passageways.[65]

To better protect vulnerable APCs, soldiers created barricades out of sandbags, the hulks of destroyed armored vehicles, and other debris to shield the vehicles when not in motion. They attached cages of wire mesh 25–30 centimeters from armor hulls to help defeat shaped charges fired against exposed vehicles. Seeking to turn Chechen anti-armor tactics against them, some units moved apparently undefended armored vehicles into ambush kill zones as bait for Chechen teams.[66] Anti-aircraft guns and helicopter gunships proved effective against ground targets. ATGMs proved capable against hardened targets. The verdict on the utility of helicopters was mixed. Although they are particularly useful for reaching upper stories of buildings, General-Colonel Vitaly Pavlov, the Russian army aviation commander, later argued that helicopters are generally not suited for urban combat.[67] Pavlov's thinking may have drawn on the demonstrated vulnerability of rotary-wing aircraft to rooftop snipers and ambushes. Nonetheless, the limited use of attack helicopters in

[65]Ibid., p. 61; Grau, *Changing Russian Urban Tactics: The Aftermath of the Battle for Grozny.*

[66]Grau, *Russian-Manufactured Armored Vehicle Vulnerability in Urban Combat: The Chechnya Experience.*

[67]Grau, *Changing Russian Urban Tactics: The Aftermath of the Battle for Grozny;* "Urban Warfare: Lessons from the Russian Experience in Chechnya 1994–1995"; Charles Heyman (ed.), *Jane's World Armies,* Jane's Information Group, 1999.

Grozny in 1994–1996 made it difficult to draw a definitive conclusion.[68]

RPO-A *Shmel* flamethrowers were the weapon of choice for the Russian troops, who referred to them as "pocket artillery." Significantly different from flamethrowers of the past, the *Shmel* is better described as a "rocket-propelled incendiary/blast projectile launcher." A single-shot, disposable weapon with a 600-meter range, the 11-kg *Shmel* is carried in packs of two. Its warhead is equipped with what the Russians call a "thermobaric" incendiary mixture. This is basically a fuel-air explosive, which upon detonation creates an expanding cloud. The cloud's ignition produces heat and overpressure with an effect comparable to that of a 152mm artillery round. The *Shmel*'s effectiveness is further enhanced by "a small hollow charge which penetrates light armor or structures to allow the main warhead to detonate inside a target." The *Shmel* had been used extensively against the tunnels and caves of Afghanistan. It proved similarly effective against the buildings and houses of Grozny.[69] There were also reports, both Chechen and Russian, that the guerrillas had acquired a handful of these weapons.[70]

Taking another page from their World War II experience, the Russians tried to emulate the assault groups or "storm" detachments of that period. This proved something of a disappointment, however, largely because the hastily assembled teams were unable to work together effectively. Because members were drawn from different units, unit cohesiveness suffered in both the assault groups and the contributing units. Commanders' complaints that the assault groups were impossible to control, however, most likely reflected a Russian military culture that had long not encouraged independent action

---

[68]"Urban Warfare: Lessons from the Russian Experience in Chechnya 1994–1995."

[69]*Jane's Infantry Weapons,* 22nd edition, 1996–1997, London, New York: Jane's Yearbooks, pp. 210–211.   "Urban Warfare: Lessons from the Russian Experience in Chechnya 1994–1995."   *Shmel: Light Flamethrower,* film, presumably Russian-produced.   According to Thomas, *The Battle of Grozny: Deadly Classroom for Urban Combat,* such a weapon was advertised for sale abroad in October 1998.   On the use of *Shmel*s in Afghanistan, see Lester W. Grau and Ali Ahmad Jalali, *Underground Combat: Stereophonic Blasting, Tunnel Rats and the Soviet-Afghan War,* Fort Leavenworth, KS: Foreign Military Studies Office Publications, *http://call.army.mil/call/fmso/fmsopubs/ issues/undrgrnd/undrgrnd.htm* (originally appeared in *Engineer,* November 1998).

[70]Jackson.

and initiative, particularly at lower levels. Thus, while a number of "storm" detachments were employed in Grozny, in other cases existing units were simply reinforced with supporting assets for assault missions. The add-on forces helped pin down the enemy while the core of the unit conducted an assault. Another approach that proved useful was sending better-trained and more experienced forces on new axes of advance. Less-seasoned soldiers could then attack from another direction and possibly have an easier time of it. This two-sided attack was hoped to minimize casualties.[71] In all cases, the basic combat element had shrunk to a manageable handful of soldiers. This was a significant improvement over the clumsy tactics of the first days of combat.

While the benefits of this restructuring far outweighed its disadvantages, there were some shortcomings. Smaller tactical units placed new strains on command, control, and coordination, especially at link-up points between units.[72] Furthermore, several other problems were never effectively resolved. The ability of the rebels to melt into the local population continued to flummox Russian soldiers, who relied on such imperfect means of differentiating combatants from noncombatants as inspecting men's shoulders for bruises, arms for singed hair, and clothes for the aftereffects of firing rounds.[73] Despite the few well-trained special troops, such as professional snipers, the force as a whole remained untrained and inexperienced. Chechens reported that one of the principal failings of Russian snipers was that they were employed as a component of the assaulting infantry, rather than out in front in a specialized and supporting, but separate, role.[74]

Overall, however, the changes in tactics and approach proved successful. Although fighting continued for some time, Russian casualty counts never again reached the levels of the first bloody days of the attack. By early March, the Russian Ministry of Defense felt suffi-

---

[71]Novichkov et al., p. 61; Grau, *Changing Russian Urban Tactics: The Aftermath of the Battle for Grozny.*

[72]Novichkov et al., p. 61.

[73]Thomas, *The Caucasus Conflict and Russian Security: The Russian Armed Forces Confront Chechnya III. The Battle for Grozny 1–26 January 1995.*

[74]Jackson.

ciently confident in its control of the city to hand it over to MVD troops for administration, leaving just a few units in the suburbs. The main part of the MoD force moved south to fight the war in the mountains.[75]

AFTER GROZNY: THE WAR CONTINUES

The capture of Grozny did not mark the end of Russian urban combat in Chechnya. Towns and villages throughout Chechnya continued to present a wide range of challenges and difficulties for the Russian forces. But it was a rebel attack on the Russian town of Budennovsk (in Russia's Stavropol region near the Chechen border) that marked the beginning of the end for Russia's Chechen campaign. On June 14, 1995, rebel commander Shamil Basaev entered the town with about 200 militia members. They first tried, and failed, to seize a police station. They were more successful in capturing two bank buildings and the city administrative center. Basaev's forces positioned machine guns on the roofs of the captured buildings and then seized the local hospital. There, they took hostages and booby-trapped the area. The rebels promised that the hostages would be released if the Russians agreed to cease hostilities in Chechnya and withdraw their forces from the region. If the Russians refused or made any attempt to resolve the situation by force, the hostages would die.

On June 17, as negotiations continued, Russian MVD and *Spetsnaz* forces attempted to recapture the hospital. *Spetsnaz* troops fired at the front windows of the hospital to create a diversion while elite Alpha group forces advanced unseen from another direction. While the Russians succeeded in temporarily capturing part of the first floor, freeing some hostages and eliminating some enemy snipers and machine gun crews, the rest of the hospital remained under Basaev's control. Two hours later they tried again, with similar results. After this second failure, Russian negotiators stated that the Russian troops were acting independently of central government control. This ended efforts to recapture the hospital and negotiations concluded on June 19. Basaev's forces may not have gotten what

---

[75]Mukhin and Yavorskiy.

they initially demanded, but they were able to return to Chechnya unimpeded, leaving behind 150 dead civilians.[76]

Budennovsk is significant for two reasons. First, Prime Minister Chernomyrdin's willingness to "appease" the hostage-takers, and to negotiate with them, significantly weakened the government's hand. Second, the government's disavowal of the efforts to recapture the hospital was guaranteed to breed resentment in the military ranks.

Russian forces faced another crisis at the end of 1995, when Salman Raduyev's Chechen fighters attacked Gudermes, Chechnya's second-largest city, believed to be firmly under Russian control. In their initial assault, Raduyev's men quickly sealed off the railroad building and the Russians' local command point. The Russians fought back with *Grad* rocket-launcher salvos and mortar attacks (they also made some use of armor). After two weeks, the fighting was at a stalemate. Rather than suffer the continuing attrition, the Russians agreed to grant Raduyev and his soldiers safe passage out of the city.[77]

In the meantime, Grozny remained fairly calm under MVD control. Early on March 6, 1996, this peace was shattered when the man responsible for Budennovsk, Shamil Basaev, and his force (estimates of his group's size vary from 150 to 1,000 men) rode directly into the Grozny central train station on a captured train. Disembarking, they fanned out toward MVD positions in northern, western, and southern Grozny. As they did, Chechen leader Djohar Dudayev broadcast a short television announcement calling for calm. The Russian forces initially responded with panic and confusion, but by the afternoon, reinforcements enabled them to contain most of Basaev's force. Even so, brutal fighting lasted five days and cost the Russians some 200 lives. In the end, Basaev's troops (accompanied by hostages they had seized) left the city in Russian hands.[78]

---

[76]Mukhin, "Military lessons of the Chechen campaign, part 6: Results of the seizure of Budennovsk by terrorists led by Shamil Basaev" (in Russian), *Nezavisimoye Voyennoye Obozreniye*, No. 243, December 26, 1996; Mukhin and Yavorskiy.

[77]Vladimir Trushkovsiy, "Terrible dispatch" [alternatively, "Dispatch from Grozny"— the Russian word "Grozny" translates as "menacing" or "terrible," as in "Ivan Grozny," known to English speakers as "Ivan the Terrible"] (in Russian), *Kommersant-Daily*, August 15, 1996.

[78]Maria Eismont, "Chechen rebels enter Grozny" (in Russian), *Segodnya*, March 7, 1996, p. 1; Dmitri Kamishev, "Situation in Chechnya" (in Russian), *Kommersant-Daily*,

If the March events proved little more than a reconnaissance by battle, Grozny's relative quiet was again shattered on August 6, 1996, by what was to be the last major action of the 1994–1996 war. It involved simultaneous Chechen attempts to recapture Grozny, Argun, and Gudermes while Russian and Chechen officials negotiated to end the conflict. In Grozny, rebel troops began infiltrating the city a few days in advance. On the morning of August 6, two 50- to 60-man units captured the railroad station and other facilities and began moving toward the center of town. Estimates of the Basaev-led force were on the order of 600 guerrillas. With reinforcements, it would eventually grow to some 4,000. The rebels succeeded in doing what the Russians had failed to do a year and a half before: they sealed off the three main avenues of approach into Grozny, restricting Russia's ability to reinforce.[79] Despite the fact that the rebels announced their intention to attack with flyers that urged Russian troops to defect and civilians to stock up on food and water and take up residence in the basements of their homes, MVD forces were apparently caught entirely unprepared. They suffered numerous casualties in the first days of fighting. The Chechens admit to a loss of 47 men in the initial attack.[80]

Ministry of Defense troops, stationed nearby in the suburb of Khankala, were not sent in to support the embattled MVD units until the second day of the battle. MoD officials, with newly appointed Defense Minister Igor' Rodionov at the helm, had been indecisive about the role of their troops in this conflict and the extent of their responsibility to support MVD forces. They were right to have been concerned: the units that finally advanced into the city from Khankala were doomed to repeat many of the events of December 1994. Many of the men who had fought the first battle of Grozny had served their terms and gone home. Those now stationed on its outskirts knew as little about urban warfare as their predecessors had two years before. Once again, maps were inadequate and troops

---

March 7, 1996; Oleg Georgiev, "Dudayev's militants attacked Grozny and acted like hardcore bandits" (in Russian), *Krasnaya Zvezda*, March 11, 1996, p. 1; Maria Eismont, "Fighting in Grozny and Sernovodsk come to an end" (in Russian), *Segodnya*, March 12, 1996, p. 1; Dmitry Zaks, "1996 Chronicle" (in Russian), *The Moscow Times*, December 31, 1996; "How it was taken."

[79]Jackson.

[80]Jackson.

unprepared. Several vehicles, including one tank, were destroyed as they drove down the narrow streets. Helicopters were ineffective and, in fact, responsible for an accidental missile strike on the local MVD headquarters. A stubborn defense of the FSB building succeeded, but at a cost of 70 soldiers' lives. On August 11, Russian armor reached the city center and, supported by artillery firing from the Khankala suburb, began the slow fight to recapture the city. By this time, however, the enemy controlled most of Grozny and was difficult to weed out. Fighting continued for nearly two more weeks. Total Russian casualties for the battle included 500 dead and 1,400 missing and wounded. When the battle finally ended, it was not with a military victory, but a cease-fire agreement finalized by negotiators Aleksandr Lebed' and Aslan Maskhadov on August 22. Their negotiations ended the war.[81]

The Russians left Chechnya having shown a surprising military weakness and lack of preparation of their forces. Moreover, many of these difficulties seemed endemic, rather than a result of a few years' decline. In the urban combat realm, the first Chechnya war demonstrated that the Russians were able to take lessons from the first days of fighting and apply them in that same battle, but seemed incapable of transmitting that knowledge beyond the soldiers and commanders responsible for developing it in the first place. Both MVD and MoD troops that fought in Grozny and other Chechen towns after February 1995 were hampered by the same problems that their compatriots had faced in December and January. While the command took some steps to improve the situation, they were insufficient. For instance, after initial losses demonstrated that predeployment training was insufficient, the Russians established training facilities for their troops in Chechnya. But a few days or weeks of drills was still inadequate training for full-fledged urban warfare. Furthermore, the Ministry of Defense's desire to rid itself of a thankless and nearly impossible mission resulted in a premature transfer of control of urban areas to MVD troops. This was a key error, as the latter forces are trained and prepared for crowd control—not positional street fighting. The MoD attitude, reflected in numerous statements at that time and since, is that domestic missions, urban and otherwise,

---

[81]Trushkovsiy; Sergei Arbuzov, "Chechnya and the army" (in Russian), *Nezavisimaya Gazeta*, August 23, 1996; Mukhin and Yavorskiy; "How it was taken."

rightly belong to someone else. Thus, the MoD was eager to leave the cities and loath to return to them, as evidenced in Grozny in August 1996.

Chapter Three

RETURN TO GROZNY: 1999–2000

STRATEGIC AND TACTICAL THINKING BETWEEN THE WARS

Although the Russians failed to institutionalize the lessons of Grozny during the war, they made a genuine effort to study its successes and failures once it was over. Most Russian analysts highlighted three key failures, one of them unique to Grozny and the other two generally applicable to the Chechen war as a whole. The first failure was that Russian forces had not effectively "blockaded" or sealed the city of Grozny prior to attack. The second failure was the poor coordination between the forces in theater, particularly the MVD and MoD. Air-ground coordination was also deficient. The third failure, discussed at length in the years after the war, was the loss of "the information war" for public opinion.

Russian planners listened to their analysts and took steps to improve coordination in the years after the war. Recognizing that problems in Chechnya were indicative of forcewide deficiencies, they developed training exercises to prepare officers and soldiers to fight within a range of force mixes and a unified command structure. Motorized rifle battalion and company officers stressed the use of artillery in their training.[1] The government granted increased authority to the military district, giving it command over all forces in its area, including MVD troops and Border Guards. "Groupings" of forces from various "power" ministries (the Russian term for all ministries with

---

[1]Aleksandr Bugai, Oleg Budula, and Viktor Shershenev, "So each would know his maneuver" (in Russian), *Krasnaya Zvezda,* Internet edition, May 4, 2000.

troops and weapons, including the MoD, MVD, FSB, Border Guards, etc.) exercised together, generally with MVD commanders assigned senior leadership roles.

The failure to seal off Grozny and other urban areas was a failure of execution rather than planning. Russian forces had intended to completely seal off the city, but failed for a number of reasons. Prior to their attack on Grozny, the Russians did not realize that small dismounted guerrilla squads presented an entirely different challenge than did the mechanized forces that Soviet encirclement norms were geared to. Encircling Grozny called for a large number of forces to cover the dozens of roads into the city. The Russians lacked the forces and the intelligence reports to carry this out prior to the New Year's Eve attack. Poor coordination between Russian forces contributed to the problem, as did a lack of individual initiative among small-unit leaders.[2]

The information war was a very different problem. Newly independent Russia's military forces had no experience with public opinion or press relations, as the Chechen war showed. They made little effort to restrict the movement of journalists in the area, so representatives of Russian and foreign newspapers, journals, and television stations had open access to the battlefield throughout the conflict. Reporters and stringers were even present on the front lines. Russian officials failed to counter their stories of a bedraggled army losing a war. Moreover, while rebel representatives eagerly granted interviews and took reporters behind their lines, Russian government and MoD officials did not. The Russian public saw the pictures on television and read the reports in the press and its support, never high to begin with, disappeared entirely as casualties mounted. Parents feared for their sons' lives, and mothers started making their way to Chechnya to take their boys home. This drew additional coverage and made the Russian military look even worse. Many in the military, and some politicians, blamed the media for the decline in public support, believing that a more "responsible" or "patriotic" press would have focused on the successes, not the failures, of the Chechnya operation. Moreover, they blamed the lack of public support for what they saw as a premature end to the war. They believed that

---

[2]Thanks to Lester Grau for his comments on this issue.

public opinion had frightened the government off and that had the war gone on, Russia would eventually have attained victory. In their view, the media was responsible for Russia's military withdrawal from its breakaway republic.[3]

But was it media coverage that alienated the Russian citizenry from this war? The conflict had never been very popular to begin with. Even the military's initial response was ambivalent. Many in the armed forces saw the war as militarily unjustifiable political adventurism. A total of 540 generals, officers, and NCOs resigned rather than serve in the 1994–1996 Chechen war.[4] It was only after heavy fighting and casualties, followed by a settlement that was negotiated with little input from the military, that veterans of the conflict began to assert that they had been betrayed.

If these three failures were what most Russian analysts saw as the root of their defeat, there were individuals both there and in the West who dug a bit deeper. These studies looked more specifically at how the Russians had fought, asking what had happened to the once mighty Red Army. It was clear that Russia's problems were more fundamental than force coordination. Rather, they were rooted in an overall low quality of troop training and competence. Even experienced troops had lacked specialized training for mountain and urban fighting—the primary terrains that the Russians faced in Chechnya. This was compounded by the last-minute formation of ad hoc groups that went to war with soldiers not knowing their comrades' names, much less feeling any real unit cohesion. Even the equipment failures that were blamed for many of Russia's woes were often a result of misuse. Existing equipment, such as mine flails, was simply not deployed in Chechnya. Similarly, reactive armor was available but not mounted on tanks that initially entered Grozny. The T-80U proved maneuverable, fast, capable of rapid fire, and invulnerable to direct fire, but it fell victim to projectiles fired from above. The older T-72 was more survivable. While the conference showed that some problems could be solved with equipment or operations modifications (e.g., replacing the T-80U gas turbine with a diesel engine and altering ammunition storage practices for armored vehi-

---

[3]See Novichkov et al.; Mukhin and Yavorskiy.

[4]Mukhin and Yavorskiy.

cles), Grozny clearly showed that most equipment failures were a result of poor training. This was a problem endemic to an under-funded conscript army and could not be corrected quickly or cheaply. Planners realized this, and they made a conscious decision to focus on a few key fixes rather than try to address every concern. Among these were force training for mountain combat, coordination between disparate forces, and the creation of a small number of permanent units manned at an 80 percent readiness level in peace-time. This last, it was hoped, would ensure the availability of capa-ble, full-strength forces when needed.[5]

There were also smaller-scale efforts to fix specific problems, such as the disappearance of some key specialties from the Russian forces. In the summer of 1999, for instance, an army directive formed a sniper training facility and manned it by competitive selection. World champion marksmen were recruited to teach small classes (the first class totaled 12 officers and soldiers) to prepare snipers for a range of operating environments.[6]

PREPARATION AND PLANNING FOR ROUND TWO

Russian efforts to change as a result of the Chechnya experience are a classic example of generals and politicians preparing to fight the last war. In this case, however, they were justified in doing so, since a rematch was coming. Key Russian military leaders like Anatoliy Kvashnin, Chief of the General Staff, were determined that this time, the fight would end in a Russian victory. Kvashnin made significant changes in Russia's exercises and planning to gear the force for "local war."[7] Few doubted that he was preparing the force for another Chechen war.

Despite the withdrawal from Chechnya, Russia maintained a signifi-cant force in the Northern Caucasus. These units specifically trained for a conflict that looked a great deal like the one that had just ended. Training and exercises were designed to support large-scale counter-

---

[5]"Russian Military Assesses Errors of Chechnya Campaign"; Michael Orr, "Second Time Lucky," *Jane's Defence Weekly*, March 8, 2000.

[6]Litovkin.

[7]Orr.

insurgency operations. An exercise in late July 1998 spanned the territories of Dagestan, North Ossetia, Ingushetia, Kabardin Balkaria, and Stavropol. MVD commanders directed some 15,000 soldiers from the MoD air, ground, and naval forces, and MVD, Border Guard, FSB, Ministry of Emergency Situations, and other forces. The exercise scenario outlined simultaneous mass attacks by "bandit" groups coupled with individual terrorist actions. A key exercise goal was cooperation and coordination among the disparate Russian forces carrying out a broad range of missions: hostage rescue, emergency response to industrial catastrophe, urban defense, attacking individual buildings, anti-terrorist actions, and more.[8]

Force restructurings, Kvashin's efforts, and well-publicized exercises belied the continued decline of Russia's military. Even as special courses honed specific skills, the average soldier or officer was getting less training. Officers complained that tank and BMP drivers and mechanics were poorly prepared, partly due to a lack of adequate training facilities.[9] Poor compliance with conscription and a lack of interest in military service led to a lack of warm bodies to fill what uniforms there were. The conscripts who reported were often poorly educated and medically unqualified. Junior officers did not stay in the service long enough to reach field-grade rank. Beginning in 1996, MoD and MVD academies began graduating students early to fill the depleted junior officer ranks.[10]

---

[8]Valentina Lezvina, "Exercises in the Caucasus" (in Russian), *Kommersant-Daily*, July 31, 1998, FBIS-UMA-98-217; Oleg Vladykin, "Dress rehearsal for war in Caucasus" (in Russian), *Obshchaya Gazeta*, August 6, 1998, p. 3, summarized in *Izvestia Press Digest*, August 6, 1998; "Northern Caucasus—region of military exercises" (in Russian), *Nezavisimoye Voyennoye Obozreniye*, July 24, 1998; Vladimir Kostrov, "Russia is making a show of force in North Caucasus" (in Russian), *Russkiy Telegraf*, July 29, 1998, p. 2, as reported by *Izvestia Press Digest*, July 29, 1998; "Major command-staff exercises underway in northern Caucasus" (in Russian), *Novosti*, Ostankino television, July 28, 1998, as reported by *East European Press Service*; "Military exercises in the northern Caucasus concluded" (in Russian), *Vesti* (Russian television), July 31, 1998, as reported by *East European Press Service*.

[9]Oleg Falichev, "Officers' gathering" (in Russian), *Krasnaya Zvezda*, Internet edition, February 22, 2000.

[10]Vladimir Gutnov, "Soldiers ask to stay in Chechnya" (in Russian), *Nezavisimoye Voyennoye Obozreniye*, Internet edition, No. 6 (179), February 18, 2000; Mukhin, "Every other youth has had no schooling" (in Russian), *Nezavisimaya Gazeta*, No. 61 (2123), Internet edition, April 5, 2000.

Despite the efforts to prepare the military to do better in a rematch with the Chechen resistance, training for urban combat was still neglected. Initial planning for the summer 1998 exercises included urban scenarios. Those were, however, eliminated in later planning, ostensibly to avoid disturbing the local population. Even the hostage-rescue scenario that remained in the exercise did not focus on engaging enemy forces in a built-up area. Instead, troops practiced for a fight in the mountains. According to one lieutenant, a recent graduate of the Leningrad Military District Academy, only a few short hours of his education had been spent on preparing for urban combat by familiarizing him and his fellow young officers with small-unit tactics and reconnaissance techniques in an urban environment.[11] Even sniper training at the new training center focused on combat in the mountains and open plains.[12]

The lack of an urban training focus was not a mistake. Rather, it reflected another conclusion military leaders had drawn from the first war in Chechnya. The blood their troops had shed in Grozny convinced Russian planners that the best approach to urban combat was to avoid it altogether. Soldiers and officers should prepare to prevent an urban fight, not to win it. Therefore, training for urban combat was deemed a waste of time and money.

Chechen incursions into Dagestan in August and September 1999 marked the beginning of the path to a second Chechen war. Public opinion against the Chechens was then further galvanized by a series of apartment bombings in Russia that same fall. While no one took responsibility for the bombings, unidentified "Chechens" were widely blamed. Initial Russian military actions in Dagestan were generally a fairly low-key effort, for although there was some fighting in and near the towns of Tando, Rakata, and Ziberhali in Dagestan and a handful of Russian attacks on fortified enemy positions, the overall focus of their mission was mining and demining, not close combat.[13] In stark contrast to the problems they had met on their way to Chechnya in 1994, Russian troops faced little or no resistance

---

[11]Falichev, "Officers' gathering."

[12]Litovkin.

[13]Aleksandr Krasnikov, "Sappers tested in 'hot spot' (in Russian), *Armeiskii Sbornik*, January 2000.

from the local inhabitants: the Dagestanis proved reluctant to join the Chechens in revolt. Moreover, unlike in 1994, the Russians took a measured and careful approach, slowly and deliberately moving through Dagestan rather than marching immediately on the Chechen capital.

After a few weeks of MVD-led operations in Dagestan, forces began to move into Chechnya itself. Here, too, they faced no significant resistance in the towns and villages of the north. Even as they moved further east, many village elders were willing to vouch for the absence of rebels in their towns to keep the troops moving along. The Russians, eager to avoid armed conflict in semi-urban areas, were willing to accept these assurances. On those few occasions when they encountered resistance, troops sealed off the town in question and bombarded it with artillery until it surrendered. Then they cleared the area, checking documents and confiscating whatever weapons they found. Finally, they turned the town over to MVD troops who set up permanent posts.[14] The imperfections of this approach were not lost on some of those participating. *Spetsnaz* personnel pointed out that village elders' promises of loyalty might mean little, as rebels could easily hide among the civilian population of a town by day and attack Russians at night.[15] But as all seemed to be going well, the Russian forces kept moving toward Grozny.

CHECHNYA BETWEEN THE TWO BATTLES FOR GROZNY: FOREIGN INVOLVEMENT AND TACTICS

According to Russian sources, the Chechen resistance was no less prepared in 1999 than it had been in 1994. According to one Russian report, Chechen leaders established a network of training centers employing some 100 foreign instructors as well as experienced Chechen fighters. One such camp was run by Khattab, an Islamic revolutionary originally from Saudi Arabia or Jordan (sources differ) who had emerged as a key Chechen commander in the first war.

---

[14]Andrei Korbut, "The Kremlin and the armed forces are learning their lessons" (in Russian), *Nezavisimaya Gazeta*, No. 37 (2099), Internet edition, February 29, 2000.

[15]Oleg Kusov, "Mood of Russian *Spetsnaz* officers in Chechnya," *Liberty Live*, Radio Liberty, January 12, 2000, *http://www.svoboda.org/archive/crisis/caucasus/0100/ll.011200-2.shtml.*

Camps had different specialties: the Alos Abudzhafar camp focused on partisan tactics and marksmanship; the Yakub camp specialized in heavy weapons; the Abubakar camp taught diversionary and terrorist tactics; and the Davlat camp taught psychological and ideological warfare. Other reports suggested that the Said ibn Abu Vakas camp in Chechnya had ties with Pakistan-based Dzhamaat Isalami (a religious-political organization whose military arm is Hizb-ul'-Mujeheddin and which also reportedly funneled money from Pakistan to the Chechen rebels) and the IIK (the Caucasian Islamic Institute, a religious/Arabic-language school with Afghan and Arab professors that is allegedly an affiliate of the Muslim Brotherhood). Russian and foreign sources alleged that these camps were financed by money from Saudi Arabia, the United Arab Emirates, Turkey, Qatar, and Jordan (perhaps unofficially) and that they hosted students from extremist organizations in Jordan, Saudi Arabia, China, Egypt, and Malaysia, as well as Palestinians from Israel.[16] Finally, Chechen field commander Salman Raduyev reportedly ran another specialized training camp called Kavkaz.[17]

The Russian press reported that Usama Bin Laden supported the Chechen rebels by sending mercenaries from Afghanistan, Yemen, and elsewhere to fight in Chechnya.[18] Pakistani groups, including Hizb-ul'-Mujeheddin and Kharakat-ul'-Mujeheddin, Al' Badr, Lashkar-e-Taiba, and Sepakhe Sakhaba Pakistan, the International Islamic Front, and Usama Bin Laden's Al' Qaida also reportedly trained and provided soldiers.[19] According to press reports, the Taliban in Afghanistan also sent men to fight alongside the

---

[16]Guria Morlinskaya, "Hot spot: Dagestan-99. Failed eden" (in Russian), *Armeiskii Sbornik*, October 1999; "Terror for export," *Krasnaya Zvezda*, Internet edition, July 7, 2000 (the article is a synopsis of a longer piece published by Vinod Anand in the June 2000 issue of the New Delhi–based Institute for Defence Studies and Analyses' monthly journal *Strategic Analysis*). All names of camps are transliterated from the Russian.

[17]Vadim Solovyov, "Federal forces' complacency does not promote the chances for a quick end to the campaign" (in Russian), *Nezavisimoye Voyennoye Obozrenniye*, Internet edition, No. 9 (182), March 17, 2000.

[18]Andrey Viktorov, "The further south, the hotter" (in Russian), *Segodnya*, December 15, 1999, Internet edition, *http://www.segodnya.ru*.

[19]"Terror for export."

Chechens.[20] It is even possible that Iraq sent specialists to help prepare defenses and build fortifications in Karabahi-Chabanmahi (in the Buynaksk region of Dagestan).[21]

As the clashes between Russian and Chechen forces in Dagestan's Botlikh region in fall 1999 demonstrated, the rebels were ready to fight, including in built-up areas. In rural terrain they camouflaged cave entrances with rocks, cobblestones, and anything else that came to hand to create shelters from artillery and air strikes. In towns and villages they used lower floors and basements of buildings as fighting positions. The rudimentary mines they laid around their battle positions convinced Russian specialists that they were professionally trained in mining operations.[22]

According to a purported Chechen guerrilla's diary published in the Russian press, Chechen actions in Dagestan were carefully planned and led by Shamil Basaev himself. Basaev divided the area into three sectors: west of Botlikh, the town of Andi, and the Gagatli area. From a total force of 5,000 men, he assigned a specific unit to each sector. Shamil Basaev commanded the main or central group, Shervani Basaev led the northern group, and Bagautdin was in charge of the southern group. Each group was subdivided into "battalions" of 50–70 people, "companies" of 15–20, and "platoons" of 5–7.[23]

THE RUSSIANS BACK IN GROZNY

The Russian approach to Grozny in 1999 was significantly different from that of 1994. The most obvious change was the long siege of the city accompanied by bombing and heavy artillery, which echoed the approach to towns in northern Chechnya that had put up resis-

---

[20]"Talibs sent reinforcements to Chechen guerrillas," *Lenta.ru*, February 1, 2000, *http://www.lenta.ru/vojna/2000/02/01/taliban/*.

[21]Krasnikov.

[22]Krasnikov.

[23]Aleksandr Kirilenko, "Guerrilla's diary," *Nezavisimoye Voyennoye Obozreniye*, No. 12 (185), Internet edition, April 7, 2000.

tance.[24] At the time, a number of Russian and Western specialists suggested that this approach, particularly the aerial attacks, emulated NATO air operations over Serbia and Kosovo during Operation Allied Force in 1999.[25] Although several Russian military officers made this argument, it is an unlikely explanation for Russian tactics. True, the two actions shared a belief that air operations could coerce enemy submission and limit the need for ground action. However, this belief was not original to either NATO or the 1990s.[26] In fact, Russian artillery bombardments of Grozny looked far more like the use of artillery in Russia's World War II campaigns than like a NATO air war. It is therefore more plausible that the Russians were not modeling their operations on NATO's, but rather employing an approach from their own history.[27]

Having reached Grozny in mid-October, the Russians settled in for several months, the bombing and artillery strikes lasting well into December. During this time troops secured key facilities in the suburbs and skirmished with rebel forces there. The Chechens, for their part, disguised themselves in Russian uniforms for night raids on Russian positions. Some of these attacks were videotaped, presumably for use as propaganda. A senior command shift from the MVD to the Ministry of Defense raised expectations that the encirclement of Grozny was a prelude to an assault on the city, but Russian military and political leaders repeatedly emphasized that they had no plans to "storm" Grozny.[28]

---

[24]"Circle around the Chechen capital is nearly closed" (in Russian), *Novosti*, Radio Station Mayak, November 2, 1999, 1500 broadcast; Maksim Stepenin, "Grozny has been divided" (in Russian), *Kommersant-Daily*, October 27, 1999, p. 3.

[25]See Sergei Romanenko, "Whose example is Russia taking?" (in Russian), *Moskovskiye Novosti*, October 5, 1999.

[26]See Robert A. Pape, *Bombing to Win: Airpower and Coercion in War*, Ithaca and London: Cornell University Press, 1996. Pape questions the efficacy of air power as a coercive instrument.

[27]E-mail exchange with BG John Reppert (ret.), December 10, 1999; Celestan.

[28]Mikhail Ragimov, "Grozny will be taken piece by piece" (in Russian), *Nezavisimaya Gazeta*, Internet edition, No. 198, October 22, 1999; Marcus Warren, "Grozny Will Be an Easy Victory, Say Russians," *London Daily Telegraph*, November 23, 1999; Aleksandr Shaburkin, "On the approaches to Grozny" (in Russian), *Nezavisimaya Gazeta*, Internet edition, November 17, 1999.

This did not, however, mean that they planned to stay out of it entirely. Russian forces probably began to enter Grozny in significant numbers in mid-December, first conducting reconnaissance-by-fire missions to determine the strength of resistance. One such action in mid-December was widely reported in the Western media as the beginning of a Russian attack on the city. Reuters correspondent Maria Eismont reported burning tanks in the streets of Grozny and over 100 Russian personnel killed. Russian officials, however, denied that they had troops in the vicinity. An independent military news agency had an alternative view, that this was a reconnaissance mission gone wrong—with far fewer killed than Eismont's estimate.[29] This seems the most likely explanation. A full attack on the city would have involved a larger force, as well as probably some immediate follow-on action.

But if the mid-December action proved a false alarm, it was clear that something was brewing as Russian authorities called on civilians to leave the city and promised safe corridors for their departure.[30] Russian motorized rifle troops faced intense enemy mortar fire as they fought to capture the airport in the Khankala suburb.[31] Despite government disavowals, by December 23 it was clear that a full-scale attack on Grozny was under way.[32]

According to official reports, the Russian attack relied heavily on a loyalist Chechen militia led by Bislan Gantamirov. Gantamirov, a

---

[29]"Grozny in the trenches" (in Russian), *SPB Vedomosti*, October 22, 1999; Viktorov, "The further south, the hotter"; "Grozny: there was no attack, was there a reconnaissance raid?" (in Russian), *Lenta.ru*, December 16, 1999, *http://lenta.ru/vojna/1999/12/16/grozny*; Maksim Stepenin, "Grozny under informational attack" (in Russian), *Kommersant-Daily*, December 17, 1999; Il'ya Maksakov, "For the first time, military actions in Chechnya diverged from political plans" (in Russian), *Nezavisimaya Gazeta*, December 17, 1999; "Russian military denied reports of artillery attack on Grozny" (in Russian), *Lenta.ru*, December 22, 1999, *http://lenta.ru/vojna/1999/12/22/grozny*; "Federal troops have parried at northern airport in Grozny" (in Russian), *Lenta.ru*, December 20, 1999, *http://lenta.ru/vojna/1999/12/20/grozny*.

[30]Petra Prokhazkova, "Heavy fighting in Grozny" (in Russian), *Novaya Gazeta*, December 20, 1999.

[31]Aslan Ramazonov and Maksim Stepenin, "Pre-New Year's storming" (in Russian), *Kommersant-Daily*, December 15, 1999; Pavel Gerasimov, "On the approaches to Grozny" (in Russian), *Krasnaya Zvezda*, December 21, 1999, Internet edition, *www.redstar.ru*.

[32]In fact, Russian officials never did admit to a "storm" of Grozny in 1999–2000.

former mayor of Grozny who had been convicted of embezzling and imprisoned in Russia, had led counter-revolutionary troops in an effort to recapture Grozny for Russia in October 1994. He had been released and pardoned to try again in 1999. Gantamirov's backers predicted victory within a week and were repeatedly credited in public statements with seizing areas and facilities in Grozny throughout December and early January. In addition to Gantamirov's militia, Russia's assault force of 4,000–5,000 men in the city proper (out of a 100,000-man deployment to Chechnya) consisted of two MVD brigades, an army regiment with associated tank, artillery, and air assets, and *Spetsnaz* components. It also included snipers, sappers, and NBC troops. The Russians estimated enemy strength in the city at about 2,000–2,500 men with a variety of weaponry at their disposal, including armored and mechanized vehicles, *Grad* rocket launchers, 152mm howitzers, 120mm mortars, and a handful of air defense missiles.[33]

Before entering Berlin 50 years ago, Russian forces had carried out a detailed study of every city block. No such effort was undertaken in advance of the attack on Grozny in 1999.[34] But planning was more detailed and preparations more advanced than they had been in 1994. Russian planners divided the city into 15 sectors. Their intent was to carry out reconnaissance in each one, followed by artillery and aviation attacks on identified resistance strongpoints, equipment, and other targets. Then, supported by mortar and sniper fire, sappers would create corridors for Russian special forces and Gantamirov's militia, who would advance toward the city center and take control of key areas. The end result would be a "spiderweb" of Russian control spanning the entire territory of the city. Within this spiderweb, motorized rifle troops organized into attack groups

---

[33]"Operation rather than storm" (in Russian), *Izvestiya*, December 23, 1999; "Federal forces in Chechnya command: fighting for Grozny will continue no less than 10 days" (in Russian), *Lenta.ru*, January 25, 2000, *http://www.lenta.ru/vojna/2000/01/25/grozny/sroki.htm*; "Has a new storm of Grozny begun?" (in Russian), *Lenta.ru*, December 23, 1999, *http://lenta.ru/vojna/1999/12/23/grozny*; "The operation to cleanse Grozny has long since begun" (in Russian), *Lenta.ru*, December 23, 1999, *http://lenta.ru/vojna/1999/12/23/grozny*; Aleksandr Sinitzin, "In Mozdok they drink to life," *Vesti.ru*, January 27, 2000, *http://vesti.ru/daynews/2000/01.27/15chechnya/*; Yuriy Zainashev, "'Souls' and RPGs" (in Russian), *Moskovskiy Komsomolets*, January 28, 2000.

[34]Falichev, "Officers' gathering."

("storm" detachments) of 30–50 men would, with air and artillery support, attack remaining enemy forces. Russian planners believed that their spiderweb would significantly limit the mobility of rebel forces, making them vulnerable to the "storm" detachments and artillery fire. Afterwards, "clearing" forces such as the Chechen loyalist militia would move into the area.[35]

The Russian "storm" detachments were geared to maximize mobility and flexibility. Within each detachment, groups of three men armed with an RPG, an automatic rifle, and a sniper rifle provided the core element. They were supported by two additional soldiers armed with automatic weapons. Other components of the "storm" group were armed with the *Shmel* RPO-A flamethrowers that had proved so effective five years before and in Afghanistan. Artillery and aviation forward observers, sappers, and reconnaissance personnel rounded out the detachment.[36]

Forces moved forward slowly and carefully in the first days of fighting. Tanks brought into the city were there to follow and support the storm detachments rather than to lead.[37] Armored vehicles moved through the city surrounded by the dismounted infantry of the attack group. The vehicles could thus effectively engage enemy snipers and automatic riflemen in the buildings that the attack troops could not reach, while being protected by the infantry who would keep the enemy from coming close enough to the armor to destroy it. Many sniper teams deployed, with the better-trained *Spetsnaz* snipers supporting the "snipers" of the motorized rifle troops, who were still basically marksmen equipped with SVD rifles.[38] Minister of Defense Igor' Sergeev focused public attention on his desire to keep casualties down: "Our predominant criteria remain the same—to

---

[35]"Operation rather than storm"; "Federal forces in Chechnya command: fighting for Grozny will continue no less than 10 days"; "Has a new storm of Grozny begun?"; "The operation to cleanse Grozny has long since begun"; Sinitzin; "Grozny trapped in 'spiderweb'" (in Russian), *Biznes & Baltia*, December 27, 1999.

[36]Andrei Mironov, "Russian forces in Chechnya using 'vacuum explosion' devices and thus violating international law" (in Russian), Radio Liberty, Liberty Live, March 18, 2000, *http://www.svoboda.org/archive/crisis/caucasus/0300/11.031800-2.shtml*; Orr; Bugai, Budula, and Shershenev.

[37]Giulietto Cieza, "In such wars there can be no victory" (in Russian), *Obshchaya Gazeta*, No. 7, Internet edition, February 17, 2000, *http://www.og.ru/mat/rep1.shtml*.

[38]Bugai, Budula, and Shershenev.

fulfill our tasks with minimal losses among the forces."[39] Forces were under orders to avoid close combat insofar as possible. To help them do so, artillery strikes preceded deliberate infantry movement into any given area.[40] First, ground troops probed deep enough to draw Chechen fire and thus expose the enemy's firing positions. The troops would then retreat to safety, calling in artillery or air strikes to destroy the enemy.[41] BMPs mounting AGS-17 automatic grenade launchers evacuated the wounded after a fight. If needed, they could simultaneously provide fire support.[42] The guiding concept seemed to be that firepower could limit the exposure of soldiers to close combat and thus save military lives, albeit at a cost to infrastructure and noncombatants.[43]

As the year drew to a close, the Russian military reported that they had broken through the first line of rebel defenses around the city perimeter. According to early reports, the forces made good initial progress toward the center of the city, advancing from three directions (northwest, west, and east).[44] Regular MVD troops were accompanied by SOBR and OMON units (MVD special forces with riot control and anti-terrorist training). Their mission was to clean up the remnants of enemy resistance.[45] Soon, Russian sources reported that MVD troops moving from the west had taken control of the Staropromislovsk region and part of the Zavod region.[46] Gantamirov's forces appeared to be rapidly approaching the city center.

---

[39]"Minister of Defense Igor' Sergeev believes that everything in Chechnya is going according to plan," *Lenta.ru*, May 1, 2000, *http://lenta.ru/vojna/2000/01/05/grozny/sergeev.htm*.

[40]Anton Maksimov, "Street fighters" (in Russian), *Ogonyok*, Internet edition, February 2000, *http://www.ropnet.ru/ogonyok/win/200060/60-10-11.html*.

[41]Mayerbek Nunayev and Richard C. Paddock, "Rebels in Chechnya Are Defending City in Ruins," *Los Angeles Times*, January 25, 2000, p. 1; Andrey Viktorov, "Crawling storm" (in Russian), *Segodnya*, December 28, 1999.

[42]Maksimov, "Street fighters."

[43] Andrei Serenko, "'Rokhlin division taking losses in Chechnya" (in Russian), *Nezavisimaya Gazeta*, Internet edition, No. 21 (2083), February 5, 2000.

[44]"Staropromislovsk section of Grozny captured by federal forces" (in Russian), *Lenta.ru*, December 31, 1999, *http://lenta.ru/vojna/1999/12/31/grozny/*.

[45]Zainashev; Aleksandr Golz, "Blitzkrieg Russian-style" (in Russian), *Itogi*, February 1, 2000.

[46]Zainashev.

By the end of December, official sources reported that the Old Sunzha region was largely under federal control as well, as was the main bridge over the Sunzha River. Russian forces were moving toward the Rodina Sovkhoz (state farm) and had reached the canning factory. According to late December press reports, all this was accomplished with no direct confrontations with enemy forces. Air power got some of the credit, with 53 sorties reportedly destroying 15 enemy strongpoints.[47]

These positive reports soon proved overly optimistic. The ease of victory had been overstated. As official forecasts of how much longer the capture of the city would take escalated from days to weeks, the fight for Grozny turned brutal. The rebel approach was similar to that of 1994–1996 and relied heavily on ambushes. Again, Russian tank columns were allowed to move down a street, only to be trapped and attacked. To the Russians' credit, the rebels were less successful with this tactic this time around. Russian sources report that only a single tank was destroyed in Grozny in 1999–2000.[48] More consistent use of reactive armor, along with dismounted infantry escort of armored vehicles, were no doubt responsible.[49] But if they had limited success destroying tanks, the rebels were still able to slow their enemy down significantly and force them into the close combat that the Russians sought to avoid. As fighting began in earnest, Russian forces were lucky if they advanced 100 meters per day. Moreover, Gantamirov's forces complained that they received little support from federal troops, who refused to come to their assistance when they were under enemy fire. Fratricide was again a problem for both the Chechen loyalists and the small armored groups that provided support for them. Furthermore, the resistance was once again more numerous and better-prepared than expected. Despite Russian claims of high enemy casualties, the guerrillas seemed only to grow in number (official estimates started at 2,000 and rose steadily to 3,000 by late January). There were strong indications that the complete encirclement of the city announced in De-

---

[47]Petr Sukhanov, "There will be no frontal confronations" (in Russian), *Nezavisimaya Gazeta*, December 30, 1999.

[48]Andrei Mikhailov, "They learned how to utilize tanks" (in Russian), *Nezavisimaya Gazeta*, No. 94 (2156), Internet edition, May 25, 2000.

[49]Prokhazkova; Bugai, Budula, and Shershenev.

cember was in fact quite porous, as the guerrillas seemed to have little difficulty reinforcing and bringing in supplies.[50]   Whatever spiderweb had been planned, actual fighting was positional and costly: house-to-house and block-by-block. Territory captured one day was lost the next.[51] Furthermore, it soon became apparent that the Russians were not, as they had hoped, shrinking the Chechen area of control as they advanced. Instead the rebels refused to be trapped and repeatedly recaptured areas, often behind Russian lines. Russian casualties continued to mount as small groups of Russian forces found that they were the ones surrounded.[52] Much of January's fighting was focused on Russian efforts to take control of the central Minutka Square, the canning plant, the bridge over the Sunzha River, and the Staropromislovsk region, all of which seemed to change hands on a daily basis if not more often.[53]

The fighting for Minutka Square was particularly bloody. Both sides sought to gain control of the "strategic heights": the taller five- and nine-story buildings ringing the square. One report from late January described a Russian unit splitting into three groups to seize three such buildings. The first (assault) group comprised the fastest, most mobile soldiers and was armed with light automatic weapons. The second (covering) group provided covering fire with heavier weaponry such as RPG-7s and machine guns. The third (support) group, which included a mortar battery, also supplied ammunition to the other two. The unit's initial effort was repulsed by fire from

---

[50]"Forces didn't manage to skip through Grozny" (in Russian), *Lenta.ru*, December 27, 1999, *http://lenta.ru/vojna/1999/12/27/grozny;* "Federal forces have recalculated the number of fighters in Grozny" (in Russian), *Lenta.ru*, January 20, 2000, *http://lenta.ru/vojna/2000/01/20/grozny.count.htm*; Zainashev; "Most important that we not be shot in the back" (in Russian), *Kommersant-Daily*, January 25, 2000.

[51]"Gantamirov's forces have reached center of Grozny" (in Russian), *Lenta.ru*, December 27, 1999, *http://lenta.ru/vojna/1999/12/27/grozny;* "Gantamirov's forces have taken Staropromislov section of Grozny" (in Russian), *Lenta.ru*, December 27, 1999, *http://lenta.ru/vojna/1999/12/27/grozny.*

[52]Andrey Matyash, "Storm of Grozny has failed" (in Russian), *Gazeta.ru*, January 6, 2000, *http://www.gazeta.ru/grozny_nostorm.shtml.*

[53]*ITAR-TASS*, January 7, 2000; *ITAR-TASS*, January 10, 2000; "Russian forces have captured several points in Grozny" (in Russian), *Lenta.ru*, January 18, 2000, *http://lenta.ru/vojna/2000/01/18/grozny/*; "Federal forces have captured Minutka Square in Grozny" (in Russian), *Lenta.ru*, January 20, 2000, *http://lenta.ru/vojna/2000/01/20/grozny/*; Anatoliy Stasovskiy, "Bandits blockaded in center of Grozny" (in Russian), *Krasnaya Zvezda*, January 20, 2000, p. 1; Golz, "Blitzkrieg Russian-style."

enemy grenade launchers and AGS-17s. Then, under cover of smokescreens, soldiers moved forward by running from one sheltering structure to another. With the help of the mortar battery, they first captured a nine-story building and then two shorter ones. Holding them proved more difficult. The taller building was soon lost to an enemy counterattack. In one of the others, the 15 Russian soldiers who had held it realized that rebel troops remained in the basement. They were ambushed when they tried to capture the rebels by pursuing them into an underground tunnel.[54]

The intensity of fighting and uncertainty of Russian control of "captured" areas made resupply a problem. Some reports indicated that occasionally materials made it through to the forces at night (this seems somewhat difficult to credit, as night movement was not the Russians' forte).[55] Russian hopes to minimize casualties by overwhelming artillery fire faltered. Instead, Russian commanders found themselves relying increasingly on snipers, which in turn made the taller buildings even more valuable. The tallest building in Grozny, a 12-story structure 500 meters from Minutka Square, became a key objective that neither side could capture. Instead, both Russian and rebel snipers took up positions in the building, from where they could hit a significant proportion of central Grozny.[56]

EVOLVING RUSSIAN APPROACHES TO URBAN COMBAT: CHANGES SINCE 1994–1995

Casualties and Morale

Despite their best efforts, the Russians could not keep casualties down as they had hoped. While official data does not break casualties down into those incurred during the fight for the capital and those who fell elsewhere, a rough estimate suggests at least 600 killed in Argun, Shali, and Grozny combined between the end of December

---

[54]Oleg Falichev, "Heavy fighting for Minutka" (in Russian), *Krasnaya Zvezda*, Internet edition, February 2, 2000.

[55]Ibid.

[56]Vasiliy Zhuchkov, "War of snipers" (in Russian), *Vremya Moscow News*, January 31, 2000.

1999 and early January 2000.[57] The true numbers are probably much higher. The 506th Motor Rifle Regiment from the Privolzhsk region lost nearly a fourth of its personnel as it fought through the outer ring of Chechen defenses in the city. This unit was subsequently replaced by the First Regiment, which continued the fight into Grozny and lost over 30 men doing so, a third of them officers. In fact, nearly half of the battalion's officer corps was killed or injured in street battles.[58] Other units suffered similar casualties. Each MVD company that first entered the city in December was 50 men strong. By the end of January many had shrunk to 20–25 men, reflecting casualties of 50 percent over the month of fighting.[59] SOBR and OMON troops took lower casualties, perhaps because these specialized forces were made up entirely of professionals rather than draftees. Furthermore, these units had experience with actions in built-up areas, if not with combat of this sort.[60]

As in 1994–1996, the high casualty rates and the difficult, manpower-intensive fight took their toll on morale. At the end of December, a reporter in Mozdok wrote that Grozny troop rotations were one week long—soldiers simply could not take any more than that. Other sources, however, reported that soldiers stayed in the city for a month at a time. Furthermore, there were numerous tales of Russian forces trading ammunition to the enemy in exchange for narcotics. They would leave the "payment" at a predetermined location, then return later to pick up the drugs, sometimes getting shot for their efforts. There were even tales of rebels buying weapons directly from Russians and paying off artillery troops not to fire. At the same time, Russian soldiers and airmen were terrified of capture; Chechen maltreatment of prisoners was notorious. Aviators reportedly flew with grenades strapped to their bodies to make sure they would not be captured alive.[61]

---

[57]Golz, "Blitzkrieg Russian-style."

[58]Vladislav Shurigin, "City of shadows" (in Russian), *APN*, February 29, 2000, *www.apn.ru/documents/2000/02/29/20000229190917.htm*.

[59]Zainashev.

[60]Zainashev; Golz, "Blitzkrieg Russian-style."

[61]Sinitzin; Bakhtiyar Ahmedakhanov, "Soldiers bargaining with own death" (in Russian), *Obshchaya Gazeta*, February 17, 2000, Internet edition, *www.og.ru/mat/ rep2.shtml*; Bugai, Budula, and Shershenev.

One major difference between this battle and the one five years before, however, was that despite cases of theft and drug abuse, most troops seemed to believe they were fighting for the good of their country. More frequent rotations and improved supply, at least in the earlier days of the battle, also contributed to better morale. The arrival of reinforcements during fighting helped as well. By mid-January 2000 a large part of the 100,000-man Northern Caucasus force, particularly its ground component, was deployed in or near Grozny.[62]

Force Coordination

Improvements in coordination between different forces are a partial success story. A single command and control system was a clear improvement. Friendly fire casualties were lower than in 1994–1995. Air operations were better synchronized with those on the ground. On the other hand, serious problems remained between MVD and MoD units and between Russian troops and Chechen loyalist militias. Some communications systems were still incompatible. MVD commanders still lacked experience using air, armor, and artillery assets. These problems were compounded by distrust among the various groups. Moreover, even with a single commander at the top, there were too many generals contributing to the confusion. Veterans reported fratricide from Russian artillery and aviation. A paratroop major who had lost 40 of his men told a journalist that "You can't even seize a building before our own howitzers start shooting at you. The pilots—those, it seems to me, have never hit a target yet."[63] But even with all of these problems, most commanders reported a much better level of coordination than in 1994–1995. If the difficulties were largely the same, the impact was smaller. Training had made a difference.

Communications

Communications also improved somewhat over the five-year interval. Improvements could largely be attributed to the deploy-

---

[62]Golz, "Front to the rear" (in Russian), *Itogi*, January 18, 2000.

[63]Golz, "Blitzkrieg Russian-style."

ment of advanced equipment, as well as better training. Special electronic warfare (EW) units were established and included in joint force groupings and subdivisions of the various forces throughout the Caucasian theater. Their primary mission was to seek out Chechen communication networks so that they could be neutralized, either physically or by jamming. Whereas in 1994–1995 the Russians were limited to a relatively narrow bandwidth, this time Russia's electronic warriors were able to operate on more frequencies. Improvements in training and equipment made it far easier for them to track the source of enemy transmissions. Outside the city, in the plains and mountains, experimental Arbalet-M radio-locational systems were deployed to pinpoint enemy locations. Arabic and Chechen interpreters were used, although there may have been shortages of these specialized personnel. Unfortunately, modern equipment often was not deployed in sufficient numbers. For instance, a helicopter-mounted EW system was deployed on only one aircraft. And if some units were trained on communications equipment, others were not. As they had five years before, Russian troops repeatedly rendered their advanced technology meaningless by communicating in the open. This enabled the rebels to evade their assaults and to ambush them.[64]

Still, overall communications improved. There were even reports of battlefield successes attributed to effective use of communications. On December 31, Colonel Evegeniy Kukarin, commander of MVD forces "East," developed and implemented EW operation "New Year." Russian troops transmitted false information over the radio to convince the rebels that an attack from the east was imminent. When the rebels reinforced in the direction of the expected attack, Kukarin's forces ambushed them, killing about 20 and wounding some 50 rebels. Kukarin was decorated as a Hero of Russia.[65]

---

[64]Vadim Koval', "Road to Gudermes" (in Russian), *Krasnaya Zvezda*, Internet edition, February 17, 1999; Vasili Gumenniy and Vladimir Matyash, "War in the airwaves," *Krasnaya Zvezda*, Internet edition, April 5, 2000.

[65]Vasiliy Panchenkov, "And battle becomes art" (in Russian), *Krasnaya Zvezda*, Internet edition, April 14, 2000.

Aviation

During the first Chechen war, reliance on flat-trajectory weapons for the bulk of the fighting resulted in heavy casualties. The alternative was to shift to high-trajectory weapons and air strikes. But the effectiveness of air and artillery varied. However brilliantly they were utilized, they were successful only insofar as they could actually destroy enemy forces. The rebel use of underground structures in the towns and cities made this particularly difficult.

Few reports from the front differentiated between air operations over cities and urban areas and those in the rest of the Chechen theater. In the war as a whole, air-ground coordination generally appeared quite effective. This was despite poor weather and smoke and fog from oil fires and fighting that sometimes precluded the effective use of combat aircraft.[66] Fixed-wing and rotary-wing aircraft were responsible for a lot of fire support. One source even suggests that they were responsible for some 80 percent of fire missions during the war, with artillery taking on another 15–17 percent, although this seems extremely high.[67] Certainly Russian pilots spent more time in the air than they were used to. On January 27, Russian forces reported 100 jet and helicopter sorties over Grozny and the southern mountains in a 24-hour period.[68] According to a report the following day, that number included flights by Su-24 and Su-25 ground-attack aircraft and Mi-24 helicopters.[69] While sortie rates were not always that high, rates of 25–60 sorties per day were normal.[70] By the middle of February, some 8,000 sorties had been flown by fixed-wing attack aircraft alone, primarily Su-24Ms and Su-25s. While these numbers are not significant by Western standards, shortages of fuel and

---

[66]Associated Press, "Russian Troops Renew Ground Attack," *International Herald-Tribune*, January 5, 2000. Evegni Pyatunin, "Masha the sniper promises to aim only for the kneecaps" (in Russian), *Nezavisimaya Gazeta*, No. 15 (2077) January 28, 2000, Internet edition, *http://www.ng.ru*.

[67]Andrei Korbut, "The Kremlin and the armed forces are learning their lessons."

[68]Associated Press, "Snipers Keep Russians Out of Grozny," *The New York Times*, January 28, 2000.

[69]Bakhtiyar Ahmedakhanov, "Victory looks ever more distinct" (in Russian), *Nezavisimaya Gazeta*, No. 15 (2077), Internet edition, January 28, 2000, *http://www.ng.ru*.

[70]Sergei Babichev, "Fighters will be gotten to even in deep holes" (in Russian), *Krasnaya Zvezda*, Internet edition, January 12, 2000.

supplies had significantly limited Russian aviators' flight hours for years. Reconnaissance aircraft, including Su-24MRs, Su-25s, MiG-25RBs, An-30Bs, and A-50s, were widely used. An-26 and Il-20 aircraft supported communications and transmitted commands. Tu-22M3 long-range bombers, however, were reportedly not used, ostensibly for fear of collateral damage (although the general Russian attitude toward collateral damage casts doubt on this explanation).[71] Of the helicopters, the Mi-24s saw considerable service, as did search and rescue Mi-8s.[72] Helicopters assumed much of the transport burden, ferrying motorized rifle troops as well as paratroopers to battle in the mountains and mountain towns.[73]

The air forces permanently deployed in the area belonged to the Fourth Air Army of the Air and Air Defense Forces. They were joined by air regiments from the Moscow Region Air and Air Defense Forces and one Central Air Force regiment. The "good news" story, as reported by air force sources, is that accuracy improved significantly from the first war, and command and control was similarly more effective. Commanders made better use of reconnaissance, and information sharing between forces and commanders increased. Air commanders had increased authority, and some reportedly refused to carry out attacks because of the risk to civilians in the area. According to aviators, fratricide did occur early in operations in Dagestan when forces were under MVD control. It was largely eliminated following the shift to MoD command. Furthermore, according to both the chief of the air forces and the commander of the Joint Aviation Group, every attack was carefully documented as a "good," or justified, strike (although some ground personnel might have disagreed with these assessments).[74]

---

[71]Sergei Sokut, "On veteran aircraft" (in Russian), *Nezavisimaya Gazeta*, No. 37 (2099), Internet edition, February 29, 2000.

[72]"Two federal helicopters shot down, one crew killed," *Lenta.ru*, December 14, 1999, *http://lenta.ru/vojna/1999/12/14/helicopters/fall.htm*; "On the first day of the new year, 200 rebels destroyed," *Lenta.ru*, January 2, 2000, *http://lenta.ru/vojna/2000/01/02/fighting.*

[73]Nabi Nabiyev, "Infantry gets wings" (in Russian), *Krasnaya Zvezda*, Internet edition, March 15, 2000.

[74]Sokut.

Aircraft and weaponry differed little from the first war. As already noted, the Su-24M remained the only widely deployed night- and foul weather–capable combat aircraft. During daylight and fair weather, it was supplemented primarily by the Su-25. The all-weather Su-25T was combat tested, and it successfully fired Kh-25ML rockets to destroy small objects such as satellite communications stations and an enemy An-2 aircraft on the ground. None of the other all-weather and night-capable fixed-wing aircraft under development in Russia were deployed to Chechnya, and there is no evidence that the GLONASS geolocational system was used at all.[75]

As in 1994–1996, unmanned aerial vehicles (UAVs) proved useful. The *Stroi*-P system, including 10 *Pchela*-1T UAVs and two ground mobile control points, deployed. The *Pchela*-1Ts could function up to 60 kilometers from their base. A successor *Pchela* system had been developed but was not deployed to Chechnya.[76]

Air-ground munitions consisted predominantly of free-fall bombs and rockets. While weapons up to 1,500 kilograms were reportedly used along with fuel-air explosives in the mountains, there were no credible reports of the use of either in Grozny. Ground fuel-air weapons such as the RPO-A *Shmel* were certainly used, however, and some experts believe that the TOS-1 Buratino, a heavy 30-barrel system mounted on a T-72 chassis (the big brother to the *Shmel*) was also employed in Grozny.[77] Precision weapons such as the KAB-500 and some air-ground missiles were employed, as well as heavy KAB-1500 L and KAB-1500 TK bombs with laser and TV sights, but not to a large extent—no more than in the 1994–1996 conflict.[78]

A final note on fixed-wing aircraft: the Russian air force suffered from a lack of qualified personnel no less than the ground forces. This was particularly true for technical specialties. Due to the lack of key technical officers, such personnel were not rotated throughout much of the fighting (as pilots were). It was not until February 2000

---

[75]Ibid.

[76]Ibid.

[77]Lester W. Grau and Timothy Smith, *A "Crushing" Victory: Fuel-Air Explosives and Grozny 2000*, Fort Leavenworth, KS: Foreign Military Studies Office Publications, *http://call.army.mil/call/fmso/fmsopubs/issues/fuelair/fuelair.htm*.

[78]Sokut; Mironov; Orr.

that additional qualified personnel were sent to the Caucasus, raising their deployment to a "wartime" level.[79]

Overall, there were two particularly significant differences between this air operation and that of the first war. One was the increased employment of air assets in general, and the other was improved coordination between aviators and ground personnel. Rotary-wing aircraft especially were far more widely used. They were responsible for almost half of the air power fire missions as well as for surveillance, delivery of personnel, extraction, and supply.[80] For the most part, helicopters were deployed throughout Chechnya as part of air tactical groups that reported to ground force commanders. These groups included two to four Mi-24 attack helicopters and one or two Mi-8 transport helicopters. In theory, their missions were coordinated by air support controllers on the ground, but the lack of trained personnel created problems. Furthermore, aviators complained that there were not enough of them deployed at the battalion level and below. Mi-24 crews often found that they got far better information from their airborne colleagues in the Mi-8s than they did from ground controllers.[81]

In addition to the air tactical group, "free hunts" by attack helicopters were conducted in the early stages of 1999–2000 Chechnya operations, perhaps comprising as much as a third of total sorties. Pairs of Mi-24 helicopters went on individual search-and-destroy missions to seek out enemy facilities and forces including firing positions, armored columns, and supply depots. Mi-24s also escorted Mi-8s on supply missions in the mountains as well as supporting the creation of barriers and zones of destruction along the roads between Itum, Kale, and Shatili. According to regulations, aircrews were required to make every effort to ensure that no civilians were present at the target site before firing.[82]

---

[79]Sokut.

[80]Dmitri Sokolov-Mitrich, "Helicopter pilot's monologue" (in Russian), *Vesti.ru*, February 10, 2000, *www.vesti.ru/pole/2000/02.10/chechnya*.

[81]Sokut; Vladimir Georgiev, "Role of Army aviation growing" (in Russian), *Nezavisimoye Voyennoye Obozreniye*, No. 4 (177), Internet edition, February 4, 2000.

[82]Sokut; V. Georgiev.

Both human and equipment problems plagued helicopter forces throughout the conflict. Ground commanders, especially (but not only) those from the MVD, were inexperienced in the use of air assets. Pilots were often forced to stay overly long on station, increasing the risk of shoot-downs. The aircraft were too old and too few. Despite plans to test night-capable Mi-24 and Mi-8 variants in Chechnya, the aircraft that were deployed generally lacked night sights and navigational equipment. Many lacked secure communications. Only five of the helicopters deployed as part of the Northern Caucasus Joint Grouping of Forces had GPS equipment (all five had previously been deployed as part of the UN force in Angola). Lacking sufficient aircraft, pilots flew their annual required hours in three months. One pilot reported logging 200 flight hours in 49 days, compared to a peacetime average of 50 hours annually. Furthermore, a lack of replacement aircraft put additional strains on repair facilities, keeping those in Mozdok running around the clock.[83]

As in the case of fixed-wing aircraft, reports of large-scale testing of new helicopters and weaponry in Chechnya seem largely unsupported. Smart bombs, such as the KAB-1500, were probably used only a handful of times. The promised new model helicopters, Ka-50 Black Sharks, never made it to Chechnya. Two Black Sharks were delivered to Mozdok in November 1999 with the expectation of more to come, but they were pulled out of the Caucasus by March 2000, having only conducted several test flights. They were never committed to combat. The new night-vision-capable Mi-24Ns finally arrived, but only in March 2000 and then in minimal numbers.[84]

Artillery

Artillery, the so-called God of War, was the basis of Russian combat in both Grozny and Chechnya as a whole in 1999–2000. Artillery was the day and night, all-weather tool for keeping the enemy at a distance and, it was hoped, for protecting Russian soldiers from close combat. Encircled towns were shelled into submission, artillery

---

[83]Sokolov-Mitrich; Cieza; Sokut; Solovyov; V. Georgiev.

[84]"Went to the mountains" (in Russian), *Profil'*, No. 10 (182), March 20, 2000, *www.profil.orc.ru/hero.html;* "'Black Sharks' frightened the Chechens" (in Russian), *Gazeta.ru*, March 10, 2000, *www.gazeta.ru/print/black_shark.shtml.*

"prepared" parts of a city or town for ground force entry, and soldiers felt comfortable calling for it whenever they met with resistance. The Russians created a strong artillery group specifically to support combat in Chechnya. Lacking a permanent readiness artillery group, the Russians cobbled this one together from a variety of sources, including artillery elements from the permanent readiness units created between the Chechnya wars. The artillery group included both conventional and rocket artillery battalions. Each ground force company had an artillery or mortar battery attached for direct support, and the Artillery and Rocket Forces commander had additional units under his command for general support. Finally, under the streamlined command and control system, junior officers had more independent authority than in previous Russian/Soviet operations to call for artillery support.[85]

Artillery systems deployed were largely the same as those in 1994–1996. Specifically, 122mm self-propelled howitzers and several types of 152mm self-propelled howitzers were used in Dagestan and Chechnya, as were the *Uragan* and *Grad* rocket systems, 82mm and 120mm mortars, and the *Nona* system (in the mountains). Multiple rocket launchers provided fire support, and the 2S19 self-propelled howitzer *Msta* did fairly well. The *Krasnopol'* precision-guided munition reportedly had consistently high accuracy (as its manufacturer had advertised before the war). Guided missile systems were used widely, and anti-tank guided missiles (PTURs) were able to destroy tanks, enemy strongpoints, and even groups of guerrillas. While officials were not keen to admit the use of surface-to-surface missiles against the rebels, the SS21 *Tochka* and *Tochka*-U systems, as well as the older R-300 SCUDs, were employed.[86] Overall, artillery proved effective, but it failed to protect Russian ground forces from close combat. Moreover, artillery bombardment of cities and towns was not enough to guarantee their pacification.

---

[85]Sokut.

[86]Sokut.

The Troops

The troops who fought in Grozny in 1999–2000 included the cream of the Russian military. Unfortunately, there was very little cream, and a good bit of skim milk had been added to the mix. Initial Russian reports claimed that almost no conscripts were sent to Chechnya, and to Grozny in particular. This was soon proved false. It is likely that because the battle for Grozny lasted longer than expected, an original intention to send only experienced men onto the urban battlefield simply proved impossible to sustain. Thus, while the personnel mix included more professional soldiers than it had five years before, inexperienced youth with perhaps three months of training still found themselves at the front.[87]

Still, this was significantly better than before. Anecdotal reports consistently reported a higher quality of professional soldier than in the last war.[88] One indicator of the poor level of preparation in 1994–1996 had been the high rate of officers killed in action compared to their men. The rebels were able to take out the leaders and scatter their soldiers fairly easily. This time around, overall casualties were similar, but officers no longer took such disproportionate losses.[89] The fact that the troops were better trained did not mean that other problems disappeared. The brutal hazing for which the Russian armed forces are infamous continued even on the front lines. One young Grozny veteran survived several battles unscathed, only to land in the hospital with a broken jaw bestowed on him by his "comrades."[90]

Specialized units deployed to reinforce the motorized rifle troops, who constituted the bulk of the Russian force and formed the basis of the attack ("storm") detachments.[91] *Spetsnaz* and paratroopers (which are separate from the air force and ground forces in Russia),

---

[87]Sergei Krapivin, "War does not have a 'parade' face" (in Russian), *Vecherniy Cheliabinsk*, January 28, 2000; Golz, "Blitzkrieg Russian-style."

[88]Igor Rotar', "Rebels remain dangerous" (in Russian), *Nezavisimaya Gazeta*, No. 47 (2109), Internet edition, March 16, 2000.

[89]Serenko; Cieza.

[90]Krapivin.

[91]Bugai, Budula, and Shershenev.

generally thought of as the most professional of Russia's combatants, were also strongly represented. Many of the more experienced forces, especially the *Spetsnaz*, had also fought in the previous Chechnya war. The Russian naval infantry (marines) also fought in Chechnya, and some of these men served in Grozny. They included both the elite "Polar Bears" of the Northern Fleet, who had developed their own training regime in preparation for battle, and a special "Black Beret" or "Scorpion" battalion assembled from all of Russia's fleets sufficiently in advance to have had the opportunity to train together before the deployment to Chechnya.[92]

"Storm" groups were employed more consistently than in 1994–1995. This time, these units were for the most part created from extant formations such as the permanent readiness groups developed in the interwar period. But last-minute ad hoc formations still occurred. For instance, a number of different platoons might be called upon to contribute individual personnel for a "storm" detachment shortly before a planned attack. The assembly of this force, whether outside the city or within city lines, was often visible to enemy forces, who were able to attack the group with AGS-17s while it was still forming up.[93] One significant difference between the two campaigns was in the allocation of greater responsibility to junior officers in 1999–2000.[94] While this was generally an improvement, inexperienced officers were often unclear in tasking subordinates. The men, in turn, were inadequately trained and had limited knowledge of terrain, and they were further hampered by unreliable communications.[95]

---

[92]Oleg Blozki, Sergey Konstantinov, Mikhail Kliment'ev, "Gathering at Grozny" (in Russian), *Izvestia*, October 22, 1999; Aleksandr Oleynik, "Every third paratrooper is fighting" (in Russian), *Nezavisimoye Voyennoye Obozreniye*, No. 48 (171), December 10, 1999, Internet edition, *nvo.ng.ru;* Kusov; Roman Fomishenko, "'Polar Bears' attack" (in Russian), *Krasnaya Zvezda*, January 12, 2000, Internet edition, *http://www.redstar.ru*; Evgeniy Ustinov, "'Scorpions' go to battle" (in Russian), *Krasnaya Zvezda*, Internet edition, March 10, 2000.

[93]Vladimir Kirichenko, "And again the battle continues . . . For those wounded in Chechnya, it is the most difficult" (in Russian), *Krasnaya Zvezda*, Internet edition, March 21, 2000.

[94]Falichev, "Officers' gathering."

[95]Ibid.

Lack of training was the bulk of the problem. But if urban combat training generally was insufficient, military leaders made a serious effort to get troops up to speed before sending them into the city. They used the suburbs of Grozny to train the five-man subgroups on how to best use cover and move around the city. The marksmen designated as "snipers" were trained as much as possible, given time constraints, in these same suburban training centers. If the Russians had avoided urban combat training between the wars, hoping that it would not be necessary, they did make real efforts to overcome that shortfall when it became clear they had no choice but to send soldiers to fight in the city.[96]

All of Russia's troops in Chechnya in 1999–2000, regardless of their service affiliation, were much better supplied than their predecessors. Soldiers had sufficient uniforms and generally received their rations. But Grozny strained supply capabilities. The longer-than-expected stay was a key factor. One commander complained to a journalist that not only was insufficient food reaching his soldiers, but there was nothing to steal from the local populace. But the fact that his troops were receiving even some supplies (cans of stew and barley porridge, according to the commander) was a tremendous improvement over the reports of starvation on the front lines in 1994–1996. Furthermore, the troops were better paid (and sometimes on time). Those in combat received 830–850 rubles daily; officers could get up to 1,000 rubles per day. (The ruble to dollar exchange rate ranged from 26 to 29 rubles to the dollar in December 1999–March 2000.) In fact, soldiers who had completed their required service occasionally chose to stay on longer to earn more money.[97] And while it is unlikely that all soldiers were so well-equipped, some were issued bulletproof vests, tourniquets, and painkillers.[98]

Logistics support in Chechnya illustrated the deficiencies of the Russian military. While supply lines did hold out well into the spring of 2000, it is unlikely that they could have done so had the war retained

---

[96]Bugai, Budula, and Shershenev.

[97]Serenko; Cieza; Golz, "Blitzkrieg Russian-style."

[98]Michael R. Gordon, "As Casualties Mount in Chechnya War, Kremlin Worries About the Political Toll," *The New York Times*, January 5, 2000, p. 1.

its intensity for much longer. The Ministry of Defense was forced to dip into its emergency reserves in order to maintain the forces, and those reserves were down to 30–35 percent by mid-March 2000.[99] Clearly, a decision had been made to ensure that the combatants were supplied, but this was at a significant cost to longer-term readiness and capability.

Night combat continued to be a problem both in the air (as already discussed) and on the ground. Night-vision equipment was sporadically issued to infantry and tank units. Although there were reports of patrols and individual night actions during the fighting for Grozny, it appears that Russian forces generally stopped fighting and hunkered down when the light faded, occasionally shooting to defend their position but doing little else. During the Grozny fighting, Russian troops usually began combat at dawn, initially advancing without artillery to gain surprise. If they were lucky, they might be able to capture one or two blocks, which they then spent the rest of the day trying to hold on to with artillery and air support. As night fell, available food and supplies were distributed and a night defense began. In mountain towns Russian forces usually just left the area at sundown, returning again the next day for "clearing" operations if there was evidence these were needed. One anecdotal report tells of harassing sniper fire in Grozny: a single armed man fired at a Russian post throughout the night. The Russians waited until well after daybreak to respond. The Chechens, on the other hand, operated effectively in the darkness, attacking isolated Russian soldiers outside their outposts. In the mountains, they entered towns as the Russians left every evening, both groups seeking rest and resupply.[100]

The Press

If artillery and aviation barrages were not a lesson Russia had taken from Western operations, the handling of the press and, through the press, of public opinion bore some resemblance to U.S. and NATO

---

[99]Solovyov.

[100]Konstantin Rashchepkin, "Komsomolskoye. Ours will capture it!" (in Russian), *Krasnaya Zvezda*, Internet edition, March 15, 2000; Milrad Fatullayev, "Komsomolskoye after the rebels and the federal troops" (in Russian), *Nezavisimaya Gazeta*, No. 61 (2123), Internet edition, April 5, 2000; Bugai, Budula, and Shershenev.

public affairs efforts during the Kosovo conflict. In fact, a government newspaper described the tight control exerted over the media as one of the few truly new aspects of national security doctrine.[101] Whereas in 1994–1996 journalists had enjoyed unimpeded access to the soldiers, the front lines, and especially to the Chechen resistance, in 1999–2000 the Russian government implemented a strict system of accreditation and escorts. At times there was a complete ban on reporters in Grozny or anywhere near Russian military forces.[102] Furthermore, while in the previous campaign there had been little effort by the Russians to "spin" the story that emerged from the conflict (in sharp contrast to the effective information campaign of the guerrillas), this time the situation was reversed. Instead of interviews with rebel leaders occupying Russia's front pages, Russian commanders and soldiers told what was largely a positive story of their success against a "terrorist" enemy. In fact, the Russian refusal to refer to the operation in Chechnya as a war, describing it instead as a "counter-terrorist operation," was largely accepted by the press. The Russian message was somewhat less clearly transmitted on the Internet, where rebel-controlled and sympathetic Web sites continued to operate.[103] The Russians, while posting regular press releases on line, did not make as extensive a use of this medium.[104]

The Russian leadership had blamed unrestricted media access for the steady decline in public support for the war in 1994–1996. Tales of young Russian soldiers starving, suffering, and dying on the front lines were reported daily in newspapers, and the corroborating images appeared nightly on televisions throughout the Russian Federation and, indeed, the world. This, combined with the lack of a clear explanation for why Russian troops were there in the first place, very likely contributed to public dissatisfaction and increased unwillingness to accept Russian casualties. This "CNN effect" was also a prob-

---

[101]*Izvestiya*, cited by Paul Goble in "A Real Battle on the Virtual Front," *RFE/RL Newsline*, Vol. 3, No. 199, part 1, October 12, 1999.

[102]Zainashev.

[103]Goble.

[104]Pavel Chernomorskiy, "Second Chechen war on the internet: Total defeat?" (in Russian), *Internet.ru*, February 18, 2000, *http://www.internet.ru/preview_a/articles/2000/02/18/1760.html.*

able factor in Russia's disinclination to send ground forces into urban combat in late 1999.

Initially, the saturation of the information nets with a pro-Russian message and strict control of journalists' access to the theater seemed to be paying off. The Russian public appeared willing, even eager, to accept the "counter-terrorist operation" as just retribution for the bombings of Russian apartment buildings, the invasion of Dagestan, and Russian failure in the last war. Reports of successful missions, brave soldiers, and low casualties helped foster this attitude and spurred Prime Minister Vladimir Putin, then acting president of Russia and the engineer behind the war machine, to increased popularity. There was even speculation that the entire conflict had been designed as a cynical ploy on Putin's part to secure the presidency in March. There is certainly reason to believe that the many somewhat premature announcements of success in both Grozny and Chechnya as a whole were at least partially driven by a desire to make the acting president and the armed forces appear effective and capable.

But as fighting dragged on from weeks into months and reports of success became less and less credible, the press began to chafe at the constraints imposed on it. The overwhelmingly positive tone of coverage at the start of the conflict slowly shifted to questioning of government reports of military successes and negligible casualty rates. Official accounts were increasingly discredited as individual soldiers and officers, interviewed when they rotated out of battle or as they lay hospitalized with injuries, told of the deaths of their comrades in engagements for which official reports had listed no losses.[105]

Furthermore, however supportive the Russian people may have been of the operation in theory, they remained broadly unwilling to send their own sons to fight.[106] Despite promises that no soldier without at least six months' experience would be sent to the front lines in Chechnya or elsewhere (another promise belied by reports from the front), even the official figures for the number of citizens failing to

---

[105]Sokolov-Mitrich.

[106]A number of female military personnel served in Chechnya in a wide variety of roles. They were, however, exclusively volunteer contract soldiers and not conscripts, as women are not subject to the draft in Russia.

report for the fall draft doubled between 1998 and 1999—from 19,600 to 38,000.[107] The Committee of Soldiers' Mothers, which came to prominence during the war in Afghanistan and spoke out in opposition to the 1994–1996 war, began keeping its own lists of casualties from Chechnya, saying that official government counts could not be trusted. These lists were published in the popular newspaper *Nezavisimaya Gazeta*.

All told, however, the media war probably could not have gone any better for the Russians than it did. The government was fairly effective in controlling media access to the front and maintaining press and public support for the war. The Russian media, like the media in most Western countries, was for the most part willing to accept both government controls and the government's story in the name of national security for as long as that story seemed plausible. The public, too, seemed happy enough at first with the government-released information. Over time, however, the disparities between the official line and the increasingly obvious reality reported by soldiers, and their parents, proved impossible to ignore. Eventually, both the press and the public became more cynical about events in Chechnya. But the propaganda campaign of the early days had done its work. Even as Russians questioned the rosy picture of how the war was going, for the most part they continued to support the operation. How long that attitude can be sustained as this conflict continues remains an open question.

THE CHECHENS STILL IN GROZNY

As in 1994, rebel forces gearing up to defend Grozny in 1999 had ample time to prepare the city. Their approach was both well thought out and professional in execution. The key to resistance operations in Grozny in 1999 was a network of underground passages. To some extent the Russians knew this and sought to counter it. Russian General-Lieutenant Gennadi Troshev (Joint Force Commander in the Northern Caucasus) stated that prior to the 1999 attack the Russian command studied not only the road system but also the sewer system, parts of which were wide enough (2–3 meters

---

[107]Mukhin, "Every other youth has had no schooling."

in diameter) for people to walk through. According to Troshev, these were mined or destroyed by Russian sappers before the bulk of his forces entered the city.[108] But events proved his assessment premature. Whatever damage Russian explosives had done, enough of the underground network survived to support the rebels consistently, even during heavy bombing and artillery attacks. This "city beneath the city" included facilities constructed in Soviet times for civil defense. Bomb shelters were used by the guerrillas as control points, rest areas, hospitals, and supply depots. Underground structures that were used in 1994–1995 were refurbished and reinforced by the rebels in the intervening years.[109] The Chechen resistance roofed some basements with concrete blocks that they could raise and lower with jacks to protect from Russian artillery strikes.[110] As was common in World War II, the guerrillas broke holes in first-floor and basement walls of adjoining buildings to create passages.[111] Despite Russian claims of a perfect seal around the city, Chechen forces were able to get in and out at several key points, such as the Old Sunzha section. These passages were used to evacuate the wounded and bring in reinforcements, weaponry, and ammunition.[112] As fighting in Grozny continued, Chechen reinforcements from outside the city were further bolstered by local residents joining the battle, some voluntarily and some under rebel coercion.[113]

In April 2000, the Russian military affairs weekly *Nezavisimoye Voyennoye Obozreniye* (Independent Military Review) published what it characterized as a captured "diary" of a Chechen guerrilla. This document outlines rebel tactics and organization throughout Chechnya, and is therefore also of interest to the analyst of Chechen

---

[108]Federal forces battle in Grozny sewers" (in Russian), *Lenta.ru*, January 28, 2000, *http://www.lenta.ru/vojna/2000/01/28/troshev/troshev.htm.*

[109]"Fighters have unimpeded access to surrounded Grozny" (in Russian), *Lenta.ru*, January 25, 2000, *http://www.lenta.ru/vojna/2000/01/25/grozny/hodyat.htm*; Il'ya Kedrov, "Ministry of Defense has brought Ministry of Internal Affairs to heel" (in Russian), *Nezavisimaya Gazeta*, No. 13 (2077), January 26, 2000, Internet edition, *http://www.ng.ru*; Bugai, Budula, and Shershenev.

[110]Kulikov.

[111]Nunayev and Paddock; Bugai, Budula, and Shershenev.

[112]Nunayev and Paddock; "Fighters have unimpeded access to surrounded Grozny."

[113]Viktorov, "'Not one step back!'—in Chechen" (in Russian), *Segodnya*, December 29, 2000.

urban operations. Whether the diary is legitimate, a piece of guerrilla disinformation, or a fabrication of journalists or Russian officials, it does appear to accurately describe many aspects of rebel actions. It paints the Chechen rebels as a highly organized force, led by a single commander and his staff, with several field commanders. During wartime, each field commander's force is split into two 500-man groupings, one active and one reserve. Five or six detachments of 100 or more personnel (the numbers don't quite add up) are each further subdivided into three fighting groups: a central, full-readiness group that remains with the commander in the mountains, a 20-man group of reconnaissance, mining, and sniper specialists deployed to a local town or village, and a support group.

Of these three, the central group has no fixed position and remains constantly on the move. Its troops all carry small arms. At the field commander's direction, they carry out raids or attacks and then move on, traveling with two radio transceivers, two pairs of binoculars, two compasses, two maps of the area, and ammunition consisting of 300 7.62mm rounds, 500–600 5.45mm rounds, 4 RPG-18 *Mukha*s, and 1,000 7.62mm PK machine gun rounds. The second group also reports to the commander, but their role is to carry out sabotage and reconnaissance missions in the towns and villages, as well as to engage in overt public affairs work, drumming up support for the resistance (however incommensurate this may seem with the sabotage and reconnaissance tasks). Finally, the support group is made up of friends and allies of the commander. They live in their own homes but remain ready to perform certain tasks at the commander's behest.

According to this diary, all Chechen guerrillas are trained in the use of several weapons including whatever Russian equipment they might capture. Training includes movement and camouflage, first aid, tactics, communications, topography, and demolition. Reconnaissance techniques and procedures are another important component of force training. Standard hand signals are used to communicate soundlessly. The diary describes rebel battle tactics as a "fleas and dogs" approach: the flea bites the dog and leaves.[114]

---

[114]Clearly a rare breed of flea.

Similarly, the guerrilla attacks and immediately moves, so as not to invite counterattack and to avoid artillery or air strikes.

The diary describes a "typical" rebel attack on an enemy post. The attack group is divided in thirds, a central force of RPG, PK, and automatic rifle gunners and two flanking groups. RPG and PK machine gunners take up supporting positions at least 50 meters away from the post. Automatic riflemen secretly approach as closely as possible and an RPG gunner initiates fire, after which the PK and RPG gunners fire steadily. The automatic rifle troops then move closer, then two flanking groups approach to a distance of 15–20 meters as the central force continues firing. The flanking groups provide cover fire as the central group moves closer to the objective. Alternatively, troops armed with automatic weapons can effect a similar advance, one group covering the other.

Turning more specifically to combat in built-up areas, the document describes the preparation of the towns and villages of Ishchersk, Goragorsk, Naursk, Alpatovo, and Vinogradnoye as defensive points in anticipation of war with Russia. The diary supports other analyses describing the rebel tactical nucleus of a 3- to 5-man fighting group, armed with some combination of a grenade launcher, a machine gun, one or two assault rifles, and a sniper rifle. A wide range of weapons, including mortars, anti-aircraft guns, KPVT and DShK machine guns, and automatic grenade launchers, are moved from point to point in the backs of civilian vehicles such as the UAZ or Jeep. Snipers generally sought to shoot first at Russian officers and "more active" soldiers. The diary notes the ease with which Russian soldiers are taken hostage, because of the lack of effective Russian base security. It relates how Russian soldiers can be persuaded to reveal sensitive information in exchange for beer or cigarettes.[115]

The diary does not address how rebel actions changed between 1994 and 2000, nor does it discuss the use of "special" weapons or information warfare. But the 1999–2000 war is notable for the increase in reports of "chemical" weapons use. While these accusations came from both sides, those of the Russians were significantly more plenti-

---

[115]Kirilenko.

ful.[116] Moreover, Russia sent NBC troops to the area and issued gas masks and other protective equipment to soldiers.[117] Military intelligence sources were quoted as saying that mines, barrels, cisterns, and canisters filled with materials such as chlorine, ammonia, liquid nitrogen, and possibly low-level radioactive waste (reportedly stolen from the Radon medical and research waste disposal facility near Grozny) had been placed at intersections of major streets. The validity of such reports is questionable, however. While fighting in and around Grozny resulted in oil spills and fire at the chemical factory, there is no proof either side used chemical weapons, even crude ones. Certainly the radioactive waste at the depository in question was an unlikely weapon. There is little radiation danger from the waste, which is at a very low level of radioactivity (although it does pose a significant environmental and public health threat if it finds its way into the soil or water). Today, according to most reports, the Radon facility is in an area under Russian control and under reliable guard.[118]

According to Vasili Gumenniy, head of the electronic warfare service of the Northern Caucasus Military Region, the Chechen communications infrastructure improved significantly over five years. While Russian government-regulated communication systems were largely absent, a collection of other systems provided more than sufficient service. The Chechens had an NMT-450 analog cellular network with two base stations, including one in Grozny. This supported communication with other locations in the Russian Federation. An AMPS station in Ingushetia provided a relay, enabling communications over the entire territory of Chechnya. Western- and Asian-made radios (Motorola, Kenwood, ICOM, and others) also provided communications. Chechen communications further included radio-relay

---

[116]"Grozny: both sides accuse each other of chemical attack" (in Russian), *Lenta.ru*, December 10, 1999, *http://lenta.ru/vojna/1999/12/10/himoruzhie/*; Sergei Mitrofanov, "Poisoned cloud of chlorine and lies," *Vesti.ru*, December 10, 1999, *http://www.vesti.ru/daynews/10-12-1999/11-grozny.htm*; "Chechen fighters using chemical weapons," *Lenta.ru*, January 1, 2000, *http://lenta.ru/vojna/2000/01/02/ chemical.*

[117]Andrei Korbut, "Chechnya: The ecological threat is growing," *Nezavisimoye Voyennoye Obozreniye*, No. 176, January 28, 2000, Internet edition, *http://nvo.ng.ru/wars/2000-01-28/2_ecohazard.html.* Blozki, Konstantinov, and Kliment'ev.

[118]"Chlorine charges defused in Chechnya" (in Russian), *Lenta.ru*, December 24, 1999, *http://lenta.ru/vojna/1999/12/24/hlor/*; Korbut, "Chechnya: the ecological threat is growing."

communications links, stationary and mobile television transmitters, short-wave radio (perhaps stolen from international organizations such as the Red Cross), "amateur" radio transmitters, and cable lines. Radios communicated in the 136–174, 300–350, and 390–470 Mhz bands, while radio/telephones communicated in the 860–960 Mhz band.[119]

If reports of cellular telephone use by the rebels in 1994–1996 were implausible, there can be little doubt that mobile phones were much in use by 1999–2000. The collapse of the telephone system in the region in the intervening period had left the area with few alternatives. According to Gumenniy, the cellular network allowed each field commander to link with a network of 20–60 individuals, while radio transmitters allowed 60–80 personnel at a time to receive intelligence data. These transmitters were often manned by prewar hobbyists who had cultivated the relevant skills and possessed the equipment to collect and transmit intelligence to support the rebels. Rebels also placed retransmitters in the mountains to extend range. Mobile INMARSAT and Iridium terminals facilitated intercity and international communications (with Egypt, Jordan, United Arab Emirates, Pakistan, Afghanistan, and Turkey) as well as providing Internet links.[120]

Leading field commanders also had television transmitters. Although their equipment was limited to a range of 20–30 kilometers, it was sufficient to transmit within a given commander's territory. Intelligence collection was aided by electronic, acoustic, radiotechnical, and radar equipment. Resistance centers of electronic reconnaissance activity were located in Grozny, Urus-Martan, Shali, Zandak, Dzhugurti, Stari Achhoy, and Shlkovskaya. Specialized Chechen troops intercepted Russian communications and transmitted false information on Russian nets.[121]

These communications improvements were the most significant change to Chechen procedures since the 1994–1996 war. The small combat group remained consistent and effective over time, hand-

---

[119]Gumenniy and Matyash.

[120]Ibid.

[121]Ibid.

held radios were still widespread, and the RPG continued to be the weapon of choice.[122] There were reports that the Chechen rebels used anti-aircraft guns against Russian ground forces in the city, as the Russians had done against the Chechens in 1994–1995. But tactics remained largely unchanged. Rebels hid in fortified basements and waited for Russian forces to get close enough to shoot, made use of underground tunnels, and looked for Russian weaknesses.[123] Unconfirmed reports said that rebel forces had acquired RPO-A *Shmel* flamethrowers and used them in Grozny and smaller towns such as Shali.[124]

Rebel air defense capability did not change significantly. One estimate suggests that the rebels began the 1999 fight with 70–100 portable air defense missiles such as the *Igla* (SA-16 "Gimlet") and used them sparingly. But even if these weapons were used rarely, they did have some effect, taking out the occasional Russian aircraft and limiting how high rotary-wing aviators were willing to fly (most tried to stay beneath 50 feet). As in the first war, Russians and Chechens both reported that the rebels had a handful of Stinger missiles. This is unlikely, as their most likely source for the missiles would have been Afghanistan, where the United States had stopped sending Stingers a decade before.[125] It is therefore generally believed that if the rebels did have any Stinger missiles, they would have been in disrepair and unusable. Other air defense weapons reportedly in the rebel arsenal included the ZSU 23-4 (*Shilka*), ZSU-2, and the *Strela-3* (SA-14 "Gremlin").[126]

Any discussion of Chechen resistance combat should include mention of the numerous reports of foreigners fighting on the Chechen side. These individuals hailed from a wide range of countries and nationalities, and reports varied on whether they were in Chechnya with or without the sanction of their home governments. Docu-

---

[122]"Staropromislovsk section of Grozny captured by federal forces"; Alice Lagnado, "Rebels 'Kill 700 Russian Troops,'" *London Times*, January 28, 2000.

[123]"Foreign press on situation in Chechnya" (in Russian), *Lenta.ru*, January 5, 2000, *http://lenta.ru/vojna/2000/01/05/grozny/abroad.htm*.

[124]Ahmedakhanov, "Soldiers bargaining with own death"; Krapivin.

[125]Sokut.

[126]Babichev; Ahmedakhanov, "Soldiers bargaining with own death."

ments purportedly found in Grozny listed such states as Sudan, Nigeria, Niger, and Ivory Coast as sending fighters to Chechnya under the guise of the International Islamic Relief Organization. Other documents listed 41 commanders in "Khatab's Islamic Company," including Jordanians, Syrians, and Pakistanis.[127] Two Chinese mercenaries were reportedly captured in Komsomolskoye.[128] While some or all of these reports may well have been Russian disinformation, there is no doubt that foreigners from all over the world came to fight in Chechnya, some for money, some in support of Islamic revolution, and others, particularly those from other former Soviet states, from hatred of Russian rule.

Most colorful were stories of the "White Stockings," female snipers from the Baltic states, Ukraine, Azerbaijan, and Russia itself, who hired themselves out to the rebels. Reports from the front said that these women were armed with VSS 9.3mm, SVD 7.62mm, and other sniper rifles. They also reportedly transmitted threats to Russian troops by radio, or promised to kill only the officers and wound the soldiers.[129] Just how many (if any) "White Stockings" actually fought in Grozny is unknown. Some journalists dismissed these stories as nothing but propaganda; others reported cases of actual shootouts with female snipers. Certainly some Russian soldiers believed the stories and spoke of their intense hatred for these "traitors."

Whatever their outside support, the Chechen rebels proved (in both 1994 and 1999) that they were not, as some had believed, random bands of irregulars. Neither were they, as General Troshev, the second in command of the Combined Force (and acting commander after Kazantsev left the theater), said, "a well-prepared professional army."[130] Rather, they were a well-prepared, reasonably well-

---

[127]"Lists of foreign mercenaries fighting in Chechnya found in Grozny" (in Russian), *Lenta.ru*, February 19, 2000, *http://www.lenta.ru/vojna/2000/02/19/archives/*.

[128]Viktorov, "Chinese mercenaries fighting with the separatists" (in Russian), *Segodnya*, Internet edition, March 10, 2000, *http://www.segodnya.ru/w3s.nsf/Contents/2000_52_news_text_viktorov1.html*.

[129]Il'ya Skakunov and Arkadiy Yuzhniy, "Bloody dowry of a Chechen Lolita" (in Russian), *Segodnya*, January 13, 2000; Natal'ya Nikulina, "Bullet in the back" (in Russian), *Slovo*, No. 11 (129), Internet edition, February 16, 2000, *http://www.slovo. msk.ru/content.html?id=766&issue=98*.

[130]Rotar'.

equipped guerrilla force defending its own territory. In many ways this proved far more dangerous to a professional army (even one in decline). The key to understanding why is asymmetry. The fundamental differences between the goals of the Russians and those of the rebels created significant advantages for the rebel force, and weakened the Russians. Where the Russians fought to control and hold territory, the rebels fought to make controlling and holding the territory as unpleasant as possible—a very different mission, and one far more difficult both to grasp and to counter. To the Russians, territory captured was territory won. To the rebels, territory lost was a temporary retreat to regroup and attack once again. This asymmetry was exacerbated by the rebels' ability to blend into the local population. Not only could the Russians not tell combatants from non-combatants, they could not tell friendly subdued territory from hostile territory teeming with enemy forces. While the rebels also preyed on weaknesses endemic to the Russian military (such as buying weapons from the soldiers and selling them drugs) their real success was in exploiting the differences between the war the Russians were fighting and their own.

THE END GAME

The asymmetric nature of the Russo-Chechen conflict helps shed light on the events of early February 2000. After weeks of heavy fighting in Grozny, on the morning of February 2 rebel forces were reported to be fleeing in droves and dying in Russian minefields. Russian officials initially responded with distrust to reports of both rebel withdrawal and deaths and injuries among the guerrilla's leadership. Presidential spokesman Sergei Yastrzhembsky voiced the general opinion: "If the guerrillas had left Grozny, there wouldn't be such fierce fighting at the cannery, the president's palace, and in the Zavodsky district." Several suggested that it was a Chechen trick or disinformation of some sort. Within days, however, the story changed. Now Russian officials spoke of a well-planned operation orchestrated by the FSB and others, an operation code-named "Wolf Hunt." An FSB agent, it appeared, had offered the beleaguered rebels a way out of Grozny in exchange for $100,000. Radio transmissions then convinced the guerrillas that Russian forces were moving from the west to the south, and a small group of rebels was allowed to successfully leave the city by the designated path. Then, when the bulk of the rebel force prepared to follow, they found that the road was mined, that Russian soldiers were everywhere, and that dozens of helicopters were shooting at them from the sky. The Russians claimed that the rebels lost up to 1,700 personnel.[131]

This story raises some questions. True, the rebels incurred significant casualties while leaving Grozny in the first days of February 2000. The wounded included leader Shamil Basaev, who subsequently had his foot amputated as a result of injuries sustained at that time. But there are inconsistencies that make it implausible that these events were entirely orchestrated by Russian forces, that the rebels left because they were losing the battle for the city, or that their losses were as high as the Russians claimed. An early February analysis, published in the *Nezavisimaya Gazeta* daily on February 5, 2000 (but presumably written before then), cited military experts who predicted that Russian forces would need until at least the end of that month to capture Grozny.[132] The confusion among the Russian leadership, the fact that the Russians were not making significant progress in the days leading up to this "retreat," the large numbers of rebels who apparently succeeded in fleeing Grozny for the mountains, and finally the estimated 1,000 rebels who remained in the city after this operation further raise questions about the plausibility of the "Wolf Hunt" story. Rebel leaders had long said they would abandon the city at some point. As spring approached, it made sense to shift operations from its ruins to the mountains, where foliage would provide cover and from where the resistance had successfully beaten back the Russians for centuries. This was what they had done five years earlier. The high casualty rates suggest that Russian intelligence had perhaps intercepted rebel withdrawal plans and used that information to persuade a number of Basaev's forces to buy their way out—into minefields and an ambush. But not

---

[131]Natalia Gorodetskaya, "Grozny Surrendered Via the Internet," *Defense and Security*, February 4, 2000; Vasiliy Zhuchkov, "Unclear Who Is Defending Grozny," *Vremya Moscow News*, February 3, 2000; Dmitri Nikolaev, "Forces heading to the mountains" (in Russian), *Nezavisimoye Voyennoye Obozreniye*, February 11, 2000; Oleg Stulov, "Wolf Hunt" (in Russian), *Kommersant-Daily*, February 5, 2000; Vladimir Galaiko, "Commander: Interview with 58th Army Commander and Hero of Russia General Vladimir Shamanov" (in Russian), *Versti*, No. 20, February 22, 2000, p. 2, as cited by *Oborona i Bezopasnost*, February 27, 2000.

[132]Serenko.

all the rebels who left took this route. Significant rebel forces had moved to the mountains, where the next phase of the war unfolded.[133]

Regardless of what happened in the lead-up to that early February 2000 ambush, the battle for Grozny was drawing to a close. Its dynamics changed significantly with the disappearance of a large part of the defensive force. While sporadic firefights continued for weeks, MoD forces began to withdraw, leaving the city largely to MVD and police control.[134]

Russian commanders declared Grozny sealed in mid-February.[135] They set up a dense network of control posts along roads leading into and through town. These varied from sandbags and cement barriers blocking the street to dug-in BTRs joined to deep parapets and trenches, with up to a company of soldiers in place. Their purpose was to monitor traffic into and out of the city and check the documents of those passing through. By mid-February, OMON troops were "clearing" the city quarter by quarter, checking documents, detaining suspicious individuals, and confiscating grenade launchers, grenades, mines, and ammunition.

Methods of identifying enemy personnel had not improved in five years' time. Russian inspectors continued to inspect men's bodies for bruises that might be caused by RPG or automatic weapons recoil. Because of the large number of posts, individuals had to submit to such checks repeatedly. But the OMON units that carried out these inspections in Grozny generally did not venture far from their well-protected posts.[136]

With the fight for the city officially over, the Emergency Ministry established soup kitchens and invited journalists to watch hungry

[133]Nikolaev.

[134]Mikhail Tolpegin, "This is no plain" (in Russian), *Segodnya*, February 8, 2000.

[135]"Grozny to be closed until April 1" (in Russian), *Lenta.ru*, February 21, 2000, *http://www.lenta.ru/vojna/2000/02/21/grozny.*

[136]Maksimov, "Road to Grozny" (in Russian), *Ogonyok*, Internet edition, February 2000, *http://www.ropnet.ru/ogonyok/win/200060/60-10-11.html;* "35 sections of Grozny cleaned" (in Russian), *Lenta.ru*, February 17, 2000, *http://www.lenta.ru/vojna/ 2000/02/17/grozny/zachistka.htm;* Rotar'.

Grozny residents line up for food. But even with the MVD ostensibly in control, sporadic fighting continued and army forces remained nearby.[137] An attack on an OMON unit near Grozny killed 20 and injured more than 30 men. It illustrated the dubious nature of government control of the area. On March 2, 2000, the OMON column was attacked as it moved through the Pervomaysk area toward the Staropromislovsky quarter of Grozny, just five kilometers outside the city. Believing the area to be safe (the quarter had surrendered without a fight during the battles for Grozny), the OMON forces were armed only with automatic rifles and communicating in the clear. They also had no armored vehicle or helicopter escort. Because they were attacked only about 200 meters from another OMON base, the troops initially thought the sound of gunfire was a welcome from their colleagues.[138]

Such attacks and other sporadic firefights continued well into April 2000, leading some to argue that few rebels had left the city after all, that the enemy had merely gone underground. The city was repeatedly closed to outside traffic, and restrictions on the press continued. Even military personnel were unable to move freely through this "liberated" city, with various restrictions imposed on when and how they could travel.[139]

URBAN OPERATIONS AFTER GROZNY: KOMSOMOLSKOYE

In 2000, as in 1995, an end to the fighting in Grozny did not mean an end to urban combat in Chechnya. The seemingly efficient path the Russian forces had cut through the towns and villages in the north of this breakaway region came back to haunt them as the war continued. Rebel attacks sprung up from the rear, from towns and areas believed "cleared" of the enemy. The attacks continued throughout the fighting in Grozny and intensified after that city was taken. Vil-

---

[137]"Went to the mountains."

[138]"OMON force from near Moscow ambushed near Grozny" (in Russian), *Lenta.ru*, March 3, 2000, *http://www.lenta.ru/vojna/2000/03/03/grozny*; Vadim Rechkalov, "We thought it was a greeting . . . " (in Russian), *Obshchaya Gazeta*, No. 10, Internet edition, March 9, 2000, *http://www.og.ru/mat/sd1.shtml*.

[139]Svetlana Nesterova, "Grozny—closed city" (in Russian), *Gazeta.ru*, April 17, 2000, *http://www.gazeta.ru/grozny_closed.shtml*.

lages in areas such as Nozhai-Yurtovsk, Veden, and Shalin reportedly remained under rebel control well into the spring of 2000.[140] The lack of confidence in government control of rear areas was reflected in warnings issued to reporters in Gudermes, who were told not to wander off and cautioned to always be accompanied by armed personnel.[141] It soon became clear that many guerrillas had never left their towns and villages as promised, but had merely shown their "civilian" face to Russian forces eager to avoid a fight. Once the Russians moved on, they were vulnerable to attack from the rear. Again and again, they had to return to fight street battles in the very towns they had "captured" without a fight.[142]

Microcosmic replays of the Grozny fighting took place in various towns in Chechnya that spring. Even in the smallest villages, aspects of the urban battlefield were present, as private homes became defensive positions.[143] Probably the bloodiest fighting took place in Komsomolskoye, a small village some 25 kilometers south of Grozny. Russian forces entered the town late on March 6 to contain rebel forces under the command of Ruslan Gelaev. Gelaev had occupied Komsomolskoye the previous day, defeating Russian motorized rifle companies (reinforced by two tanks) on its outskirts. Rebel snipers provided cover for their forces as they entered the town. Even after the Russians sent in an Alpha special forces sniper unit from the Western Grouping, the rebels continued to reinforce and did not back down.[144]

Once Russian forces and rebel forces were both in Komsomolskoye proper, the situation worsened. The estimated 600–1,000 rebels who had initially broken through into the village were bolstered by the local villagers, who had clearly been planning for this fight for some time. Carefully engineered defenses were in place, including a sys-

---

[140]Bahtiyar Ahmedhanov, "Uniform without honor" (in Russian), *Obshchaya Gazeta*, No. 14, Internet edition, April 6, 2000, *http://www.og.ru/mat/rep2.shtml.*

[141]Rotar'.

[142]Golz, "Front to the rear."

[143]Nabiyev, "Infantry gets wings."

[144]Liz Fuller, "Pitched Battle Under Way South of Grozny," *RFE/RL Newsline*, Vol. 4, No. 37, Part I, February 22, 2000; Rashchepkin, "How Komsomolskoye was freed" (in Russian), *Krasnaya Zvezda*, Internet edition, April 16, 2000.

tem of underground structures similar to that in Grozny.[145] The familiar reinforced basements were sometimes supplemented by additional "wells" dug beneath them. Teams of two or three men, armed with RPGs and machine guns, repeatedly emerged from these shelters to attack Russian forces with short-range massed fire, then retreated to their underground bunkers. Russian troops lobbed grenades into basements but generally found that rebels would throw them back before they exploded. Several Russian tanks and BTRs were destroyed, one when an explosive was thrown directly into its open hatch. As in Grozny, tanks were generally used to provide fire support for the MVD forces, sometimes by simply moving down the narrow streets firing continuously. General-Major Grigoriy Fomenko, the commander of the MVD Western Grouping, brought in more armor as the fighting continued. Two tanks and a *Shilka* (ZSU 23-4) self-propelled anti-aircraft gun system were sent to destroy enemy strongpoints in the town. They failed, and the lead tank was destroyed by a rebel RPG.

The Russian approach in Komsomolskoye was, once again, massive artillery and air strikes followed by dismounted forces, predominantly MVD but with some MoD personnel for support. Supporting fire utilized artillery, tanks, surface-to-surface missiles, attack helicopters, and bombers, the latter flying day and night missions. Su-24 bombers and Su-25 ground-attack aircraft, however, were hampered by the proximity of Russian troops to enemy forces. Although reports of the use of the *Buratino* TOS-1 fuel-air system in Grozny were difficult to confirm, it seems clear that this weapon was used in Komsomolskoye. Armored and mechanized vehicles included MoD tanks and MVD BTRs. Dogs were brought in to find mines and assist in searches. As in Grozny, Russian ground forces generally did not move after dark, returning instead to safe positions and barricading themselves in captured houses.[146]

---

[145]Solovyov; Nabiyev, "Their final goal was Urus-Martan" (in Russian), *Krasnaya Zvezda*, Internet edition, March 20, 2000; Viktorov; Rashchepkin, "How Komsomolskoye was freed."

[146]Lema Turpalov, "Valerik [river of death] of the end of the 20th century" (in Russian), *Nezavisimaya Gazeta*, No. 67 (2129), Internet edition, April 13, 2000; Andrei Mironov; Orr; "Hunt for Gelayev results in nothing" (in Russian), *Lenta.ru*, March 16, 2000, *http://www.lenta.ru/vojna/2000/03/15/baranov/*.

The fighting in Komsomolskoye lasted three weeks, the rebels successfully reinforcing from the mountains throughout that time. Even toward the end, when they controlled only a handful of houses, Chechen forces continued to fight intelligently and capably, constantly shifting position. In the end, the Russians claimed to have killed 500 enemy fighters, but exact tallies were impossible because the guerrillas had been diligent in evacuating their dead and wounded. Civilian casualties were deemed to be few in number, as most of the noncombatant residents had fled. But if the Russians "saved" this town, it was by destroying it. By the time the fighting was over, there was little left.[147]

Komsomolskoye is significant for the same reasons that the Budennovsk and Grozny battles of 1995 and 1996 were significant. While it is clear that the Russian forces in the city of Grozny in 1999–2000 were better prepared than their predecessors, this did not translate into improved urban fighting capability for the Russian armed forces as a whole. A lack of focus on this form of warfare, stemming largely from a continued refusal to accept it as a possibility, had the same effect this time as the last. Once again, Russian soldiers were unprepared for the real dangers and difficulties of attacking a fortified populated area. Once again, the rebels were better prepared, better trained, and more motivated. If little armor was lost in Grozny, the tanks that burned in the little village of Komsomolskoye cast a dark shadow on that accomplishment. That here, as in the larger city, the end result was the almost complete destruction of the village, in part with the powerful fuel-air explosive TOS-1, is significant for both a better understanding of urban combat and our appraisal of Russia's capabilities.

---

[147]Shaburkin, "Fighting continues in Komsomolskoye" (in Russian), *Nezavisimaya Gazeta*, No. 46 (2108), Internet edition, March 15, 2000; Rashchepkin, "Komsomolskoye. Ours will capture it!" Vasili Fatigarov, "On the ruins of the bandits' nest" (in Russian), *Krasnaya Zvezda*, Internet edition, March 21, 2000; Turpalov; Rashchepkin, "How Komsomolskoye was freed."

Chapter Four

CONCLUSIONS

RUSSIA'S CAPABILITIES 1994–2000: LESSONS LEARNED AND LESSONS FORGOTTEN

Many who looked at the first Chechen conflict, and at Russian forces in Grozny in that time frame, saw that campaign as the final proof of the Russian military's demise. Hungry, ill-trained troops dying by the hundreds in an effort to subdue a renegade province do not make for good press. Conversely, tales of Russian success in 1999–2000 are read by some as a signal of Russia's resurgence, the first step toward its return to claim the mantle of the USSR. Both assessments are exaggerated, polarized views. While neither is completely true, however, both have elements of accuracy.

In both wars, Chechnya and Grozny showed that there are a number of things Russia's military can do reasonably well. The Russian armed forces can, for instance, deploy and command forces as necessary to carry out a local war. At the tactical level, the Russian military showed it can learn from mistakes and adapt. The adjustments in tactics after the first bloody days of 1995 were a forceful example of flexibility under unfavorable circumstances. Individual Russian commanders and soldiers also showed themselves capable of quick thinking, improvisation, and bravery. Organizationally, the Russian defense establishment proved that it can adapt, as it did in creating readiness brigades. As phrased by Minister of Defense Sergeev, the fact that soldiers went to war with their units, rather than getting to know each other "in the tank or BMP," was key to the success of operations.[1] Better training for specialized forces and for troops destined for mountain combat, as well as all-round better preparation, no doubt had a significant impact. Joint operations exercises involving various forces and services also made a difference. Perhaps even more important were the mutually supportive roles laid out for ground forces, MVD, and other troops as well as for their subcomponents, and the fact that all of them reported to a single commander. All these factors testify to the Russian military's ability to make real changes. The increased effectiveness they fostered demonstrates that Russia is capable of real military reform.

But if the Russian military can learn and adapt in both the short and long term, it seems to have more trouble in the intermediate term. While forces on the ground responded to the situation around them, and careful study yielded significant changes over the interwar period, the Russians seemed to forget painfully learned lessons from one battle to the next. If Russian urban fighting ability improved during the first battle for Grozny, leaders were unable to transfer that knowledge to those who had to defend the city a few short months later. They were able to capture the well-defended city again half a decade later, but they seemed to have forgotten everything they had learned about enemy fortifications and tactics by the time they entered the town of Komsomolskoye.

Furthermore, if the Russians improved on some aspects, they ignored others. Due to a lack of training and equipment, most Russian forces cannot fight effectively at night. They continue to have trouble with secure voice communications. Aging and decrepit equipment is an ever-increasing problem. Time and again, they failed in basic military skills, such as carrying out reconnaissance to determine enemy strength. This problem was highlighted in Grozny in 1994, 1996, and 1999, as well as in Komsomolskoye in 2000.

If training and equipment remained a problem, planning in 1999–2000 was much improved. There was a reasonable war plan for Grozny (albeit one based on expectations of a much lower level of resistance than proved to be the case). The Russian military learned from its own mistakes, history, and its enemy in switching to and

---

[1] Falichev, "Officers' gathering."

planning for small-unit tactics. Combat in Grozny in 1999–2000 benefited tremendously from new approaches to force protection. While armor protection proved more effective than did the effort to avoid close combat through heavy artillery use, the fact that such issues had been considered is an important indicator of the sort of planning that had been absent five years before. Unlike in 1994–1995, force ratios reflected the terrain and the conflict. The Russians recognized the disadvantages of being the attacker and increased their forces accordingly (although their failure to estimate enemy strength accurately meant that the ratios in Grozny still fell short of those prescribed by Soviet World War II doctrine). In stark contrast to 1994, the troops who entered Grozny in 1999 were a sizable force, reasonably well-supplied, that had the benefit of better training. A unified chain of command ensured that air and artillery support would be forthcoming and that different forces knew their missions. Most important, they had a plan for capturing Grozny, and they had commanding officers whose orders were clear on the need to avoid casualties.

Another success of 1999–2000 was a direct outgrowth of what the Russian leadership saw as a failure of 1994–1996. Control of the press this time around was stringent, and the Russians got their side of the story out. The high public approval ratings for the war as it continued bore out the benefits of this approach. While over time the media became increasingly dissatisfied with the situation, and criticism emerged at home and abroad, the fact is that the Russian defense establishment ran an effective media campaign, one largely in keeping with a modern military force seeking to safeguard the details of its operations. There is no question that Russia also had an interest in minimizing any reports of failure, of higher-than-expected casualties, or of human rights violations, but that, too, is not unusual for a modern military embarking on a campaign (although the extent of both casualties and human rights violations reported in the second Chechnya campaign still remained well above levels that most Western militaries might tolerate). Insofar as was possible in a society that at the time enjoyed a relatively free press, the Kremlin and the Ministry of Defense did quite well in maintaining support for the 1999–2000 Chechnya campaign.

If in 1994–1996 the military campaign in Chechnya in general and Grozny in particular demonstrated the deterioration of the Red Army from its days of glory, the conflict in 1999–2000 equally clearly demonstrated that reports of Russia's military demise had been, to paraphrase Samuel Clemens, premature. The Russian armed forces were able to deploy, reinforce, and supply a corps-sized force to fight a significant local conflict. They could plan and carry out plans effectively. Despite some problems, the Russian armed forces showed proficiency in combined arms operations. Finally, and most important, both in 1994 and all the more so in 1999, Russia was able to demonstrate that despite their scanty training and limited military education, its soldiers, marines, and airmen could still engage in combat effectively.

LEARNING FROM THE RUSSIAN EXPERIENCE

In spite of the better planning, improved training, reasonably effective force coordination, and a successful media campaign, Russian forces took heavy casualties in Grozny and, through their tactics, virtually destroyed the city. Even then, it is unclear whether the rebels' retreat was a result of genuine Russian victory or of previously laid guerrilla plans.

Thus, whatever else the Russian army proved itself capable of in Chechnya and Grozny over the last five years, it could not and cannot bloodlessly and effectively capture a large urban area from an insurgent force. One reason for this limitation is that in 1999, as in 1994, the Russians were fundamentally unprepared for urban combat. Forces practiced for mountain combat, for small-scale counterterrorist actions, even for urban defense, but not for capturing a populated area by force. True, the Russians developed real plans and paid some attention to training their soldiers. They also made careful and seemingly effective preparations for the attack, including encircling and cutting off the city. But the plans once again failed to take into account the possibility of real resistance, and most of the training the soldiers received took place on the outskirts of Grozny itself only days before they were sent in. Moreover, despite all efforts, the encirclement proved porous.

Why, in preparing for a second large-scale Chechnya war, did the Russians fail to prepare for a second major battle for the city of Grozny? On the basis of the evidence assembled in this report, the failure stemmed from the Russians' fervent hope of not needing to engage in another round of urban combat. All other lessons aside, the one thing the Russians had truly learned from the nightmare of 1994–1995 was that urban combat was to be avoided at all costs. Fighting in a city was difficult, bloody, and very manpower-intensive. It was the quickest way possible to send hundreds of body bags home to Russian parents. It was the most difficult and unlikely way imaginable to attain the sort of quick military success that played well in the media and with the electorate. The Russian military leadership therefore decided to avoid close combat altogether. Its forces would instead bypass towns and make deals with village elders. They would shell Grozny, and any smaller towns that proved recalcitrant, into submission.

They soon found that this approach was flawed. The Russian military was unable to avoid urban combat in Grozny, Komsomolskoye, and a range of smaller towns.[2] Because the Russians so feared urban combat, and were so determined to avoid it, they were largely unprepared for it when it came.

In 1994 the Russians had ignored all evidence that a Chechen resistance remained in Grozny. In 1999 they convinced themselves that weeks of aerial bombardment had driven the rebels out.[3] The guerrillas purposely made it appear that way; certainly it was in their interests to draw the Russians into a city where significant resistance remained and the rebels could do what they did in 1994. The result was similar: significant Russian casualties and a drawn-out battle to capture and hold every block of territory.

The Russians faced a very difficult enemy in Chechnya. An insurgent force on its home territory is a very different thing from a conventional army. The enemy can melt back into the population. Village elders can lie when they assure troops of their town's loyalty. Most important, because the two sides are fighting very different wars, the insurgents have an easier template for victory. The Russians had to win and hold territory. The Chechens just had to make doing so sufficiently painful that their enemy would give up the task.

---

[2] Korbut, "The Kremlin and the armed forces are learning their lessons."

[3] Golz, "Front to the rear."

The urban dimension makes things even more complicated, combining the advantages of insurgency with those of defense. Sealing off a city, with its many streets and underground passageways, is difficult even for planners who know it well, and it consumes vast amounts of manpower. Surrounding the city is not enough. And once fighting begins, its complex terrain of streets, buildings, and other structures provides every advantage to the defender who knows his city. In Grozny, furthermore, the rebels were able to augment these advantages with modern technology. The small groups of rebels moved rapidly underground and through the lower stories of buildings, using hand-held radios to keep in constant contact with their leaders. As a result, the rebels had a far clearer sense of the battlefield than did the Russians, and even with overwhelming numbers and overwhelming firepower, the Russians were able to attain their questionable victory only with high casualties and only by destroying much of the city.

How, then, can a modern and capable force train for such contingencies? A careful study of the tactics of both sides in Grozny is an excellent start. A commitment to training forces for a wide range of contingencies in built-up areas is equally imperative. Understanding the advantages of the defense is essential. The biggest mistake one can make is the one the Russians made between 1996 and 1999: By believing that they could avoid urban battle by not preparing for it, the Russian military guaranteed that any fight, successful or otherwise, would have a very high cost.

BIBLIOGRAPHY

Books, Monographs, and Articles

"35 sections of Grozny cleaned" (in Russian), *Lenta.ru,* February 17, 2000, *http://www.lenta.ru/vojna/2000/02/17/grozny/zachistka.htm.*

Ahmedakhanov, Bakhtiyar, "Soldiers bargaining with own death" (in Russian), *Obshchaya Gazeta,* February 17, 2000, Internet edition, *www.og.ru/mat/rep2.shtml.*

———, "Uniform without honor" (in Russian), *Obshchaya Gazeta,* No. 14, Internet edition, April 6, 2000, *http://www.og.ru/mat/rep2.shtml.*

———, "Victory looks ever more distinct" (in Russian), *Nezavisimaya Gazeta,* No. 15 (2077), Internet edition, January 28, 2000, *http://ng.ru.*

Arbuzov, Sergei, "Chechnya and the army" (in Russian), *Nezavisimaya Gazeta,* August 23, 1996.

Babichev, Sergei, "Fighters will be gotten to even in deep holes" (in Russian), *Krasnaya Zvezda,* Internet edition, January 12, 2000.

"'Black Sharks' frightened the Chechens" (in Russian), *Gazeta.ru,* March 10, 2000, *http://www.gazeta.ru/print/black_shark.shtml.*

Blozki, Oleg, Sergey Konstantinov, and Mikhail Kliment'ev, "Gathering at Grozny" (in Russian), *Izvestia,* October 22, 1999.

Bugai, Aleksandr, Oleg Budula, and Viktor Shershenev, "So each would know his maneuver" (in Russian), *Krasnaya Zvezda,* Internet edition, May 4, 2000.

Celestan, Gregory J., *Wounded Bear: The Ongoing Russian Military Operation in Chechnya,* Fort Leavenworth, KS: Foreign Military Studies Office Publications, 1996, downloaded from *http://call.army.mil/call/fmso/fmsopubs/issues/wounded/wounded. htm.*

"Chechen fighters using chemical weapons," *Lenta.ru,* January 1, 2000, *http://lenta.ru/vojna/2000/01/02/chemical.*

Chernomorskiy, Pavel, "Second Chechen war on the internet: total defeat?" (in Russian), *Internet.ru,* February 18, 2000, *http://www.internet.ru/preview_a/articles/2000/02/18/1760.html.*

"Chlorine charges defused in Chechnya" (in Russian), *Lenta.ru,* December 24, 1999, *http://lenta.ru/vojna/1999/12/24/hlor.*

Cieza, Giulietto, "In such wars there can be no victory" (in Russian), *Obshchaya Gazeta,* No. 7, Internet edition, February 17, 2000, *http://www.og.ru/mat/rep1.shtml.*

"Circle around the Chechen capital is nearly closed" (in Russian), *Novosti,* Radio Station Mayak, November 2, 1999, 1500.

Eismont, Maria, "Chechen rebels enter Grozny" (in Russian), *Segodnya,* March 7, 1996, p. 1.

———, "Fighting in Grozny and Sernovodsk come to an end" (in Russian), *Segodnya,* March 12, 1996, p. 1.

Falichev, Oleg, "Officers' gathering" (in Russian), *Krasnaya Zvezda,* Internet edition, February 22, 2000.

——— "Heavy fighting for Minutka" (in Russian), *Krasnaya Zvezda,* Internet edition, February 2, 2000.

Fatigarov, Vasili, "On the ruins of the bandits' nest" (in Russian), *Krasnaya Zvezda,* Internet edition, March 21, 2000.

Fatullayev, Milrad, "Komsomolskoye after the rebels and the federal troops" (in Russian), *Nezavisimaya Gazeta*, No. 61 (2123), Internet edition, April 5, 2000.

"Federal forces battle in Grozny sewers" (in Russian), *Lenta.ru*, January 28, 2000, *http://www.lenta.ru/vojna/2000/01/28/troshev/troshev.htm*.

"Federal forces in Chechnya command: fighting for Grozny will continue no less than 10 days" (in Russian), *Lenta.ru*, January 25, 2000, *http://www.lenta.ru/vojna/2000/01/25/grozny/sroki.htm*.

"Federal forces have captured Minutka Square in Grozny" (in Russian), *Lenta.ru*, January 20, 2000, *http://www.lenta.ru/vojna/2000/01/20/grozny*.

"Federal forces have recalculated the number of fighters in Grozny" (in Russian), *Lenta.ru*, January 20, 2000, *http://lenta.ru/vojna/2000/01/20/grozny.count.htm*.

"Federal troops have parried at northern airport in Grozny" (in Russian), *Lenta.ru*, December 20, 1999, *http://lenta.ru/vojna/1999/12/20/grozny*.

Fel'gengauer, Pavel, "Generals should not be berated, but rather retrained" (in Russian), *Segodnya*, December 25, 1996.

"Fighters have unimpeded access to surrounded Grozny" (in Russian), *Lenta.ru*, January 25, 2000, *http://www.lenta.ru/vojna/2000/01/25/grozny/hodyat.htm*.

Fomishenko, Roman, "'Polar Bears' attack" (in Russian), *Krasnaya Zvezda*, January 12, 2000, Internet edition, *http://www.redstar.ru*.

"Forces didn't manage to skip through Grozny" (in Russian), *Lenta.ru*, December 27, 1999, *http://lenta.ru/vojna/1999/12/27/grozny*.

"Foreign press on situation in Chechnya" (in Russian), *Lenta.ru*, January 5, 2000, *http://lenta.ru/vojna/2000/01/05/grozny/abroad.htm*.

Fuller, Liz, "Pitched Battle Under Way South of Grozny," *RFE/RL Newsline*, Vol. 4, No. 37, Part I, February 22, 2000.

Galaiko, Vladimir, "Commander: Interview with 58th Army Commander and Hero of Russia General Vladimir Shamanov" (in Russian), *Vesti*, No. 20, February 22, 2000, p. 2, as cited by *Oborona i Bezopasnost*, February 27, 2000.

"Gantamirov's forces have reached center of Grozny" (in Russian), *Lenta.ru*, December 27, 1999, *http://lenta.ru/vojna/1999/12/27/grozny*.

"Gantamirov's forces have taken Staropromislov section of Grozny" (in Russian), *Lenta.ru*, December 27, 1999, *http://lenta.ru/vojna/1999/12/27/grozny*.

Georgiev, Oleg, "Dudayev's militants attacked Grozny and acted like hardcore bandits" (in Russian), *Krasnaya Zvezda*, March 11, 1996, p. 1.

Georgiev, Vladimir, "Role of Army aviation growing" (in Russian), *Nezavisimoye Voyennoye Obozreniye*, No. 4 (177), Internet edition, February 4, 2000.

Geranin, Vasiliy, "Terrible lessons of Grozny" (in Russian), *Armeyskiy Sbornik*, May 1998, pp. 22–24.

Gerasimov, Pavel, "On the approaches to Grozny" (in Russian), *Krasnaya Zvezda*, December 21, 1999, Internet edition, *www.redstar.ru*.

Goble, Paul, "A Real Battle on the Virtual Front," *RFE/RL Newsline*, Vol. 3, No. 199, Part 1, October 12, 1999.

Golz, Aleksandr, "Blitzkrieg Russian-style" (in Russian), *Itogi*, February 1, 2000.

———, "Front to the rear" (in Russian), *Itogi*, January 18, 2000.

Gordon, Michael R., "As Casualties Mount in Chechnya War, Kremlin Worries About the Political Toll," *The New York Times*, January 5, 2000, p. 1.

Gorodetskaya, Natalia, "Grozny Surrendered via the Internet," *Defense and Security*, February 4, 2000.

Grau, Lester W., *Changing Russian Urban Tactics: The Aftermath of the Battle for Grozny*, Fort Leavenworth, KS: Foreign Military Studies Office Publications, 1995, downloaded from *http://call.army.mil/call/fmso/fmsopubs/issues/grozny.htm*. Originally published as "Russian Urban Tactics: Lessons from the Battle for Grozny," *INSS Strategic Forum*, No. 38, July 1995.

——, *Russian-Manufactured Armored Vehicle Vulnerability in Urban Combat: The Chechnya Experience*, Fort Leavenworth, KS: Foreign Military Studies Office Publications, downloaded from *http://call.army.mil/call/fmso/fmsopubs/issues/rusav/rusav.htm* (originally appeared in *Red Thrust Star*, January 1997).

——, and Ali Ahmad Jalali, *Underground Combat: Stereophonic Blasting, Tunnel Rats and the Soviet-Afghan War*, Fort Leavenworth, KS: Foreign Military Studies Office Publications, downloaded from *http://call.army.mil/call/fmso/fmsopubs/issues/undrgrnd/undrgrnd.htm* (originally appeared in *Engineer*, November 1998).

——, and Timothy Smith, *A "Crushing" Victory: Fuel-Air Explosives and Grozny 2000*, Fort Leavenworth, KS: Foreign Military Studies Office Publications, downloaded from *http://call.army.mil/call/fmso/fmsopubs/issues/fuelair/fuelair.htm*.

"Grozny: both sides accuse each other of chemical attack" (in Russian), *Lenta.ru*, December 10, 1999, *http://lenta.ru/vojna/1999/12/10/himoruzhie*.

"Grozny in the trenches" (in Russian), *SPB Vedomosti*, October 22, 1999.

"Grozny: there was no attack, was there a reconnaissance raid?" (in Russian), *Lenta.ru*, December 16, 1999, *http://lenta.ru/vojna/1999/12/16/grozny*.

"Grozny to be closed until April 1" (in Russian), *Lenta.ru*, February 21, 2000, *http://lenta.ru/vojna/2000/02/21/grozny*.

"Grozny trapped in 'Spiderweb'" (in Russian), *Biznes & Baltia*, December 27, 1999.

Gumenniy, Vasili, and Vladimir Matyash, "War in the airwaves," *Krasnaya Zvezda*, Internet edition, April 5, 2000.

Gutnov, Vladimir, "Soldiers ask to stay in Chechnya" (in Russian), *Nezavisimoye Voyennoye Obozreniye*, Internet edition, No. 6 (179), February 18, 2000.

"Has a new storm of Grozny begun?" (in Russian), *Lenta.ru*, December 23, 1999, *http://lenta.ru/vojna/1999/12/23/grozny*.

Heyman, Charles (ed.), *Jane's World Armies*, Jane's Information Group, 1999.

"How it was taken" (in Russian), *Vremya Moscow News*, February 7, 2000.

"Hunt for Gelayev results in nothing" (in Russian), *Lenta.ru*, March 16, 2000, *http://www.lenta.ru/vojna/2000/03/16/baranov*.

Jackson, Timothy, *David Slays Goliath: A Chechen Perspective on the War in Chechnya (1994–1996)*, Appendix C, "Chechen Technique for Urban Ambushes," Marine Corps Warfighting Lab, 2000.

Jane's Infantry Weapons, 22nd edition, 1996–1997, London, New York: Jane's Yearbooks, pp. 210–211.

Kamishev, Dmitri, "Situation in Chechnya" (in Russian), *Kommersant-Daily*, March 7, 1996.

Kedrov, Il'ya, "Ministry of Defense has brought Ministry of Internal Affairs to heel" (in Russian), *Nezavisimaya Gazeta*, No. 13 (2077), January 26, 2000, Internet edition, *http://www.ng.ru*.

Kirichenko, Vladimir, "And again the battle continues . . . For those wounded in Chechnya, it is the most difficult" (in Russian), *Krasnaya Zvezda*, Internet edition, March 21, 2000.

Kirilenko, Aleksandr, "Guerrilla's diary," *Nezavisimoye Voyennoye Obozreniye*, No. 12 (185), Internet edition, April 7, 2000.

Korbut, Andrei, "Chechnya: The ecological threat is growing," *Nezavisimoye Voyennoye Obozreniye*, No. 176, January 28, 2000, Internet edition, *http://nvo.ng.ru/wars/2000-01-28/2_ecohazard.html*.

————, "The Kremlin and the armed forces are learning their lessons" (in Russian), *Nezavisimaya Gazeta*, No. 37 (2099), Internet edition, February 29, 2000.

Kostrov, Vladimir, "Russia is making a show of force in North Caucasus" (in Russian), *Russkeiy Telegraf*, July 29, 1998, p. 2, as reported by *Izvestia Press Digest*, July 29, 1998.

Koval', Vadim, "Road to Gudermes" (in Russian), *Krasnaya Zvezda*, Internet edition, February 17, 1999.

Krapivin, Sergei, "War does not have a 'parade' face" (in Russian), *Vecherniy Cheliabinsk*, January 28, 2000.

Krasnikov, Aleksandr, "Sappers tested in 'hot spot'" (in Russian), *Armeiskii Sbornik*, January 2000.

Kulikov, Anatoly S., "The First Battle of Grozny," in Russell W. Glenn (ed.), *Capital Preservation: Preparing for Urban Operations in the Twenty-First Century—Proceedings of the RAND Arroyo-TRADOC-MCWL-OSD Urban Operations Conference, March 22–23, 2000*, Santa Monica, CA: RAND, CF-162-A, 2001.

Kusov, Oleg, "Mood of Russian *Spetsnaz* officers in Chechnya," Liberty Live, Radio Liberty, January 12, 2000, *http://www.svoboda.org/archive/crisis/caucasus/0100/ll.011200-2.shtml*.

Lagnado, Alice, "Rebels 'Kill 700 Russian Troops,'" *London Times*, January 28, 2000.

Lambeth, Benjamin S., *Russia's Air Power at the Crossroads*, Santa Monica, CA: RAND, 1996.

Lezvina, Valentina, "Exercises in the Caucasus" (in Russian), *Kommersant-Daily*, July 31, 1998, FBIS-UMA-98-217.

"Lists of foreign mercenaries fighting in Chechnya found in Grozny" (in Russian), *Lenta.ru*, February 19, 2000, *http://www.lenta.ru/vojna/2000/02/19/archives*.

Litovkin, Dmitri, "Sniper signature," *Krasnaya Zvezda*, Internet edition, April 14, 2000.

Loshak, Viktor, "Second-rate people behind the wheel of the army" (in Russian), *Moskovskiye Novosti*, No. 9 (1026), Internet edition, March 7–13, 2000, *http://www.mn.ru/2000/09/71.html*.

"Major command-staff exercises underway in northern Caucasus" (in Russian), *Novosti*, Ostankino television, July 28, 1998, as reported by *East European Press Service*.

Maksakov, Il'ya, "For the first time, military actions in Chechnya diverged from political plans" (in Russian), *Nezavisimaya Gazeta*, December 17, 1999.

Maksimov, "Road to Grozny" (in Russian), *Ogonyok*, Internet edition, February 2000, *http://ropnet.ru/ogonyok/win/200060/60-10-11.html*.

———, "Street fighters" (in Russian), *Ogonyok*, Internet edition, February 2000, *http://www.ropnet.ru/ogonyok/win/200060/60-10-11.html*.

Matyash, Andrey, "Storm of Grozny has failed" (in Russian), *Gazeta.ru*, January 6, 2000, *http://www.gazeta.ru/grozny_nostorm.shtml*.

Mikhailov, Andrei, "They learned how to utilize tanks" (in Russian), *Nezavisimaya Gazeta*, No. 94 (2156), Internet edition, May 25, 2000.

"Military exercises in the northern Caucasus concluded" (in Russian), *Vesti* (Russian television), July 31, 1998, as reported by *East European Press Service*.

"Military lessons of the Chechen campaign: the Grozny operation" (in Russian), *Oborona i Bezopasnost'*, No. 133–134, November 11, 1996.

"Military lessons of the Chechen campaign: preparation for the beginning of military actions (December, 1994)" (in Russian), *Oborona i Bezopasnost'*, October 23, 1996.

"Minister of Defense Igor' Sergeev believes that everything in Chechnya is going according to plan," *Lenta.ru*, May 1, 2000, *http://lenta.ru/vojna/2000/05/01/grozny/sergeev.htm*.

Mironov, Andrei, "Russian forces in Chechnya using 'vacuum explosion' devices and thus violating international law" (in Russian), Radio Liberty, Liberty Live, March 18, 2000, *http://www.svoboda.org/archive/crisis/caucasus/0300/11.031800-2.shtml.*

Mitrofanov, Sergei, "Poisoned cloud of chlorine and lies," *Vesti.ru*, December 10, 1999, *http://www.vesti.ru/daynews/10-12-1999/11-grozny.htm.*

Morlinskaya, Guria, "Hot spot: Dagestan-99. Failed eden" (in Russian), *Armeiskii Sbornik*, October 1999.

"Most important that we not be shot in the back" (in Russian), *Kommersant-Daily*, January 25, 2000.

Mukhin, Vladimir, "Every other youth has had no schooling" (in Russian), *Nezavisimaya Gazeta*, No. 61 (2123), Internet edition, April 5, 2000.

———, "Military lessons of the Chechen campaign, part 6: results of the seizure of Budennovsk by terrorists led by Shamil Basaev" (in Russian), *Nezavisimoye Voyennoye Obozreniye*, No. 243, December 26, 1996.

———, "Military lessons of the Chechen campaign, part 8: the fight in Grozny in August 1996, the end of military operations," *Nezavisimaya Gazeta*, January 25, 1997.

———, and Aleksandr Yavorskiy, "War was lost not by the army, but by politicians" (in Russian), *Nezavisimaya Gazeta—Osobaya Papka*, Internet edition, No. 37 (2099), February 29, 2000.

Nabiyev, Nabi, "Infantry gets wings" (in Russian), *Krasnaya Zvezda*, Internet edition, March 15, 2000.

———, "Their final goal was Urus-Martan" (in Russian), *Krasnaya Zvezda*, Internet edition, March 20, 2000.

Nesterova, Svetlana, "Grozny—closed city" (in Russian), *Gazeta.ru*, April 17, 2000, *http://www.gazeta.ru/grozny_closed.shtml.*

Nikolaev, Dmitri, "Forces heading to the mountains" (in Russian), *Nezavisimoye Voyennoye Obozreniye*, February 11, 2000.

Nikulina, Natal'ya, "Bullet in the back" (in Russian), *Slovo*, No. 11 (129), Internet edition, February 16, 2000, *http://www.slovo.msk. ru/content.html?id=766&issue=98.*

"Northern Caucasus—region of military exercises" (in Russian), *Nezavisimoye Voyennoye Obozreniye*, July 24, 1998.

Novichkov, N. N., et al., *The Russian armed forces in the Chechen conflict: analysis, results, conclusions* (in Russian), Paris, Moscow: Kholveg-Infoglob, Trivola, 1995.

Nunayev, Mayerbek, and Richard C. Paddock, "Rebels in Chechnya Are Defending City in Ruins," *Los Angeles Times*, January 25, 2000, p. 1.

Oleynik, Aleksandr, "Every third paratrooper is fighting" (in Russian), *Nezavisimoye Voyennoye Obozreniye*, No. 48 (171), December 10, 1999, Internet edition, *http://nvo.ng.ru.*

"OMON force from near Moscow ambushed near Grozny" (in Russian), *Lenta.ru*, March 3, 2000, *http://www.lenta.ru/vojna/2000/ 03/03/grozny.*

"On the first day of the new year, 200 rebels destroyed," *Lenta.ru*, January 2, 2000, *http://lenta.ru/vojna/2000/01/02/fighting.*

"Operation rather than storm" (in Russian), *Izvestiya*, December 23, 1999.

"The operation to cleanse Grozny has long since begun" (in Russian), *Lenta.ru*, December 23, 1999, *http://lenta.ru/vojna/1999/12/23/ grozny.*

Orr, Michael, "Second Time Lucky," *Jane's Defence Weekly*, March 8, 2000.

Panchenkov, Vasiliy, "And battle becomes art" (in Russian), *Krasnaya Zvezda*, Internet edition, April 14, 2000.

Pape, Robert A., *Bombing to Win: Airpower and Coercion in War*, Ithaca and London: Cornell University Press, 1996.

Prokhazkova, Petra, "Heavy fighting in Grozny" (in Russian), *Novaya Gazeta*, December 20, 1999.

Pyatunin, Evegni, "Masha the sniper promises to aim only for the kneecaps" (in Russian), *Nezavisimaya Gazeta*, No. 15 (2077), January 28, 2000, Internet edition, *http://www.ng.ru.*

Raevsky, Andrei, "Chechnya: Russian Military Performance in Chechnya: An Initial Evaluation," *Journal of Slavic Military Studies*, December, 1995, p. 682.

Ragimov, Mikhail, "Grozny will be taken piece by piece" (in Russian), *Nezavisimaya Gazeta*, Internet edition, No. 198, October 22, 1999.

Ramazonov, Aslan, and Maksim Stepenin, "Pre–New Year's storming" (in Russian), *Kommersant-Daily*, December 15, 1999.

Rashchepkin, Konstantin, "How Komsomolskoye was freed" (in Russian), *Krasnaya Zvezda*, Internet edition, April 16, 2000.

———, "Komsomolskoye. Ours will capture it!" (in Russian), *Krasnaya Zvezda*, Internet edition, March 15, 2000.

Rechkalov, Vadim, "We thought it was a greeting . . . " (in Russian), *Obshchaya Gazeta*, No. 10, Internet edition, March 9, 2000, *http://www.og.ru/mat/sd1.shtml.*

Romanenko, Sergei, "Whose example is Russia taking?" (in Russian), *Moskovskiye Novosti*, October 5, 1999.

Rotar', Igor, "Rebels remain dangerous" (in Russian), *Nezavisimaya Gazeta*, No. 47 (2109), Internet edition, March 16, 2000.

"Russian forces have captured several points in Grozny" (in Russian), *Lenta.ru*, January 18, 2000, *http://lenta.ru/vojna/2000/01/18/grozny.*

"Russian Military Assesses Errors of Chechnya Campaign," *Jane's International Defense Review*, April 1, 1995.

"Russian military denied reports of artillery attack on Grozny" (in Russian), *Lenta.ru*, December 22, 1999, *http://lenta.ru/vojna/1999/12/22/grozny.*

"Russian Troops Renew Ground Attack," Associated Press, *International Herald-Tribune*, January 5, 2000.

Serenko, Andrei, "Rokhlin division taking losses in Chechnya" (in Russian), *Nezavisimaya Gazeta*, Internet edition, No. 21 (2083), February 5, 2000.

Shaburkin, Aleksandr, "On the approaches to Grozny" (in Russian), *Nezavisimaya Gazeta*, Internet edition, November 17, 1999.

———, "Fighting continues in Komsomolskoye" (in Russian), *Nezavisimaya Gazeta*, No. 46 (2108), Internet edition, March 15, 2000.

Shmel: Light Flamethrower, film, presumably Russian-produced.

Shurigin, Vladislav, "City of shadows" (in Russian), *APN*, February 29, 2000, *www.apn.ru/documents/2000/02/29/20000229190917.htm*.

Sinitzin, Aleksandr, "In Mozdok they drink to life," *Vesti.ru*, January 27, 2000, *http://vesti.ru/daynews/2000/01.27/15chechnya*.

Skakunov, Il'ya, and Arkadiy Yuzhniy, "Bloody dowry of a Chechen Lolita" (in Russian), *Segodnya*, January 13, 2000.

"Snipers Keep Russians Out of Grozny," Associated Press, *The New York Times*, January 28, 2000.

Sokolov-Mitrich, Dimitri, "Helicopter pilot's monologue" (in Russian), *Vesti.ru*, February 10, 2000, *http://www.vesti.ru/pole/2000/02.10/chechnya*.

Sokut, Sergei, "On veteran aircraft" (in Russian), *Nezavisimaya Gazeta*, No. 37 (2099), Internet edition, February 29, 2000.

Solovyov, Vadim, "Federal forces' complacency does not promote the chances for a quick end to the campaign" (in Russian), *Nezavisimoye Voyennoye Obozreniye*, Internet edition, No. 9 (182), March 17, 2000.

"Special Report, The Chechen Conflict: No End of a Lesson?" *Jane's Intelligence Review*, September 1, 1996.

Speyer, Arthur L. III, "The Two Sides of Grozny," in Russell W. Glenn, (ed.), *Capital Preservation: Preparing for Urban Operations in the Twenty-First Century—Proceedings of the RAND Arroyo-TRADOC-MCWL-OSD Urban Operations Conference, March 22–23, 2000*, Santa Monica, CA: RAND, CF-162-A, 2001.

"Staropromislovsk section of Grozny captured by federal forces" (in Russian), *Lenta.ru*, December 31, 1999, *http://lenta.ru/vojna/1999/12/31/grozny*.

Stasovskiy, Anatoliy, "Bandits blockaded in center of Grozny" (in Russian), *Krasnaya Zvezda*, January 20, 2000, p. 1.

Stepenin, Maksim, "Grozny has been divided" (in Russian), *Kommersant-Daily*, October 27, 1999, p. 3.

Stepenin, Maksim, "Grozny under informational attack" (in Russian), *Kommersant-Daily*, December 17, 1999.

Stulov, Oleg, "Wolf Hunt" (in Russian), *Kommersant-Daily*, February 5, 2000.

Sukhanov, Petr, "There will be no frontal confrontations" (in Russian), *Nezavisimaya Gazeta*, December 30, 1999.

"Talibs sent reinforcements to Chechen guerrillas," *Lenta.ru*, February 1, 2000, *http://www.lenta.ru/vojna/2000/02/01/taliban*.

Taysumov, Bakar, "On the eve of a metropolitan clash" (in Russian), *Nezavisimaya Gazeta*, February 6, 1997.

"Terror for export," *Krasnaya Zvezda*, July 7, 2000.

Thomas, Timothy, *The Battle of Grozny: Deadly Classroom for Urban Combat*, Fort Leavenworth, KS: Foreign Military Studies Office Publications, downloaded from *http://call.army.mil/call/fmso/fmsopubs/issues/battle.htm* (originally appeared in *Parameters*, Summer 1999, pp. 87–102).

———, *The Caucasus Conflict and Russian Security: The Russian Armed Forces Confront Chechnya III. The Battle for Grozny 1–26 January 1995*, Fort Leavenworth, KS: Foreign Military Studies Office Publications, downloaded from *http://call.army.mil/call/fmso/fmsopubs/issues/chechpt3.htm* (originally appeared in *Journal of Slavic Military Studies*, Vol. 10, No. 1, March 1997, pp. 50–108).

Tolpegin, Mikhail, "This is no plain" (in Russian), *Segodnya*, February 8, 2000.

Trushkovsiy, Vladimir, "Terrible dispatch" [alternatively, "Dispatch from Grozny"] (in Russian), *Kommersant-Daily,* August 15, 1996.

Turpalov, Lema, "Valerik [river of death] of the end of the 20th century" (in Russian), *Nezavisimaya Gazeta,* No. 67 (2129), Internet edition, April 13, 2000.

"Two federal helicopters shot down, one crew killed," *Lenta.ru,* December 14, 1999, *http://lenta.ru/vojna/1999/12/14/helicopters/fall.htm.*

"Urban Warfare: Lessons from the Russian Experience in Chechnya 1994–1995," *http://www.geocities.com/Pentagon/6453/chechnyaA.html.*

Ustinov, Evgeniy, "'Scorpions' go to battle" (in Russian), *Krasnaya Zvezda,* Internet edition, March 10, 2000.

"Victory looks ever more distinct" (in Russian), *Nezavisimaya Gazeta,* No. 15 (2077), Internet edition, January 28, 2000, *http://www.ng.ru.*

Viktorov, Andrey, "Chinese mercenaries fighting with the separatists" (in Russian), *Segodnya,* Internet edition, March 10, 2000, *http://www.segodnya.ru/w3s.nsf/Contents/2000_52_news_text_viktorov1.html.*

———, "The further south, the hotter" (in Russian), *Segodnya,* December 15, 1999, Internet edition, *http://www.segodnya.ru.*

———, "'Not one step back!'—in Chechen" (in Russian), *Segodnya,* December 29, 2000.

Vladykin, Oleg, "Dress rehearsal for war in Caucasus" (in Russian), *Obshchaya Gazeta,* August 6, 1998, p. 3, summarized in *Izvestia Press Digest,* August 6, 1998.

Warren, Marcus, "Grozny Will Be an Easy Victory, Say Russians," *London Daily Telegraph,* November 23, 1999.

"Went to the mountains" (in Russian), *Profil',* No. 10 (182), March 20, 2000, *http://www.profil.orc.ru/hero.html.*

Yavorskiy, Aleksandr, "Pilots not given time to turn around" (in Russian), *Nezavisimoye Voyennoye Obozreniye,* December 10, 1999.

Yefimov, G. P., "Features of the Defense of Large Cities and Industrial Areas," *Military Thought*, January 1, 1990.

Zainashev, Yuriy, "'Souls' and RPGs" (in Russian), *Moskovskiy Komsomolets*, January 28, 2000.

Zaks, Dmitry, "1996 Chronicle," *The Moscow Times*, December 31, 1996.

Zhuchkov, Vasiliy, "Unclear who is defending Grozny," *Vremya Moscow News*, February 3, 2000.

———, "War of snipers" (in Russian), *Vremya Moscow News*, January 31, 2000.

News Coverage

Gazeta.ru

ITAR-TASS

Jamestown Foundation Monitor

Krasnaya Zvezda

Lenta.ru

Nezavisimaya Gazeta

Nezavisimoye Voyennoye Obozreniye

Radio Free Europe/Radio Liberty Newsline (RFE/RL Newsline)

Segodnya

Reference Books and Databases

Cullen, Tony, and Christopher F. Foss (eds.), *Jane's Land-Based Air Defence, 10th Edition, 1997–1998*, Jane's Information Group, 1997.

Foss, Christopher F. (ed.), *Jane's Armour and Artillery, 20th Edition, 1999–2000*, Jane's Information Group, 1999.

Hogg, Ian V. (ed.), *Jane's Infantry Weapons, 19th Edition, 1993–1994,* Jane's Information Group, 1993.

Jackson, Paul MRAeS (ed.), *Jane's World Air Forces,* Jane's Information Group, 1999.

Periscope database, *http://www.periscope.ucg.com/index.shtml.*

Additional Resources

Author e-mail exchanges with BG John Reppert (ret.), Executive Director (Research) for the Belfer Center for Science and International Affairs, John F. Kennedy School of Government at Harvard University, and former U.S. Defense Attaché to Russia.

Author conversations with Timothy Thomas, Foreign Military Studies Office, Fort Leavenworth, Kansas.

http://members.nbci.com/082499/aviation/chechnya/101499.htm.

http://www.military.cz/russia/air/suchoj/Su_37/su_37.htm.